The Gourmand

D1500595

Don't eat anything your great-grandmother
wouldn't recognise as food.

MICHAEL POLLAN
FOOD RULES: AN EATER'S MANUAL (2009)

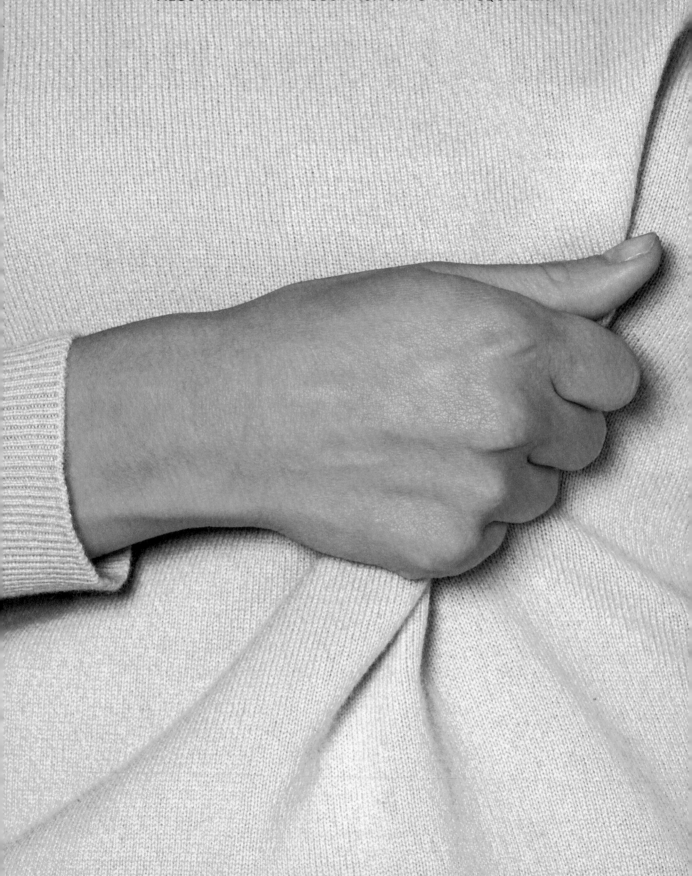

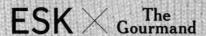
ESK ✕ The Gourmand

'ENGLISH MUSTARD' CASHMERE SWEATER BY ESK X THE GOURMAND
WOMEN'S CHLOE ROUND NECK AND MEN'S DEE CREW NECK
ALSO AVAILABLE IN 'SCOTTISH OATS' AND 'SQUID INK'

ESKCASHMERE.COM · THEGOURMAND.CO.UK

Editors-in-Chief
David Lane & Marina Tweed

Editor
Ananda Pellerin

Creative Director
David Lane

Contributing Editor
Patrick Baglee

Contributing Writers
Patrick Baglee
Louise Benson
Sam Bompas
Clare Considine
Ben Houston
Kyle Hugall
Takamasa Kikuchi
Scarlett Kilcooley-O'Halloran
Kelly MacLean
Antto Melasniemi
Ananda Pellerin
Kingston Trinder
Tom Viney

Contributing Illustrators
Klaus Haapaniemi
Jean Jullien
Tim Lahan
Jo Ratcliffe

Cover Image: Still from a 16mm Film by
Director • Lisa Rovner
Director of Photography • Jeremy Valender
Hair & Makeup • Ruth Coutinho
Gaffer • Grzegorz Krzeszowiec
Models • Sion & Tiffany Phillips
Production • Gelardin Management

**Contributing Stylists
& Set Designers**
Julian Ganio
Peta O'Brien
Gemma Tickle

Contributing Photographers
Jess Bonham
Jason Evans
Luke Evans
Ernst Fischer
Adrianna Glaviano
Julia Grassi
Carl Kleiner
Benjamin McMahon
Lisa Rovner
Bronia Stewart
Yann Stofer
Aaron Tilley

Marketing Associate
Thomas Scalé

Designer
Bruce Usher

Designer
Oliver Long

Publishing Assistant
Taahir Husain

Sub-Editing
Helius

Thank You
Ace Hotel • Agi & Sam Studio • AI PR • Julian Aicher • Andy at Sable's • Thorbjorn Ankerstjerne • Baker & Evans
Edward Benson • Juliet Benson • Jackson Berg • Betsy • Betty • Massimo Bottura • Bulthaup • Ally Capellino • Neneh Cherry
Ryan Chetiyawardana • Cinelab • Ruth Coutinho • Doogie • ESK • Rupert Evans-Harding • Frank • Gelardin Management
Jody Ghanem • Lara Gilmore and all the staff at Osteria Francescana • Simon Gregory • Bernd Grether
Julia Hanisch • Anya Hindmarch • Harmony Hubick • Freddie Jannsen • Kettle's Yard • Hilary Lane MBE • Susan Langan
The Liberace Foundation for the Creative and Performing Arts • James Lowe • Bettina Loycke • Masumi sake
John McCarthy at Labyrinth Photographic • Brad McDonald • Emma McIntyre • Cameron McVey • Mabel McVey • Jonathan Meades
Kathrin Mühlhofer • Moschino • Virginia Norris • PG Film & Commercial • Sion Phillips • Tiffany Phillips • Nicholas Russell
Tom Sansome • Tom Scalé • Ruth Segarra • Paul Smith • Andrew Stellitano • Charlie Thomas • Jeremy Valender • Vitsoe • Minni Von Podewils
Oliver Waddington-Ball at The Tuck Shop, Goldfinger Factory • Molly Wansell • Penny Watson • 75 Wanted

Distribution
The Gourmand is distributed internationally through independent
bookshops, boutiques, galleries and department stores, and online.
We work closely with established partners such as Antenne Books and MMS.
For all distribution or stocking enquiries please contact: info@thegourmand.co.uk

Published by The Gourmand Ltd
94 De Beauvoir Rd
London N1 4EN
thegourmand.co.uk

lecturis
printing company

The Gourmand is printed
in the Netherlands
by Lecturis Printing Company

The Gourmand

Monotype

The Gourmand is typeset in
Gourmand Grotesque & Cheltenham BT,
both from Monotype

Ally Capellino

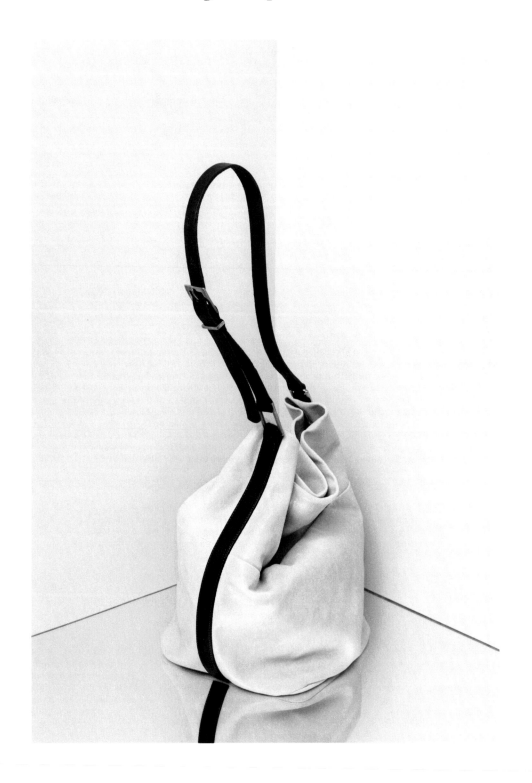

Contributors

Patrick Baglee is a Cumbrian, a writer and a Fellow of the Royal Society of Arts.

Louise Benson is associate editor at Postmatter.com, where she covers innovations in art, design, fashion and science. She is also working on a personal project about London's airports.

Sam Bompas is one half of Bompas & Parr, and co-author of *Feasting with Bompas & Parr*. In the past he's worked with jelly, built a boating lake on the roof of Selfridges, created a walk-in cloud of breathable cocktail and hosted the multisensory fireworks for London's New Year's Eve celebrations.

Jess Bonham is a London-based still-life photographer. Working with a diverse range of collaborators, she has been commissioned by clients including Kenzo, Selfridges, Belvedere, Ford, Jaguar, Aston Martin, British *Vogue*, *Twin*, *Wired*, *Wonderland* and *Garage*.

Clare Considine is a London-based culture writer for the likes of *The Guardian Guide*, *The Word* and *Stylist*. She writes a lot about music and thinks a lot about food.

Jason Evans is a Welsh photographer based in Ramsgate. Smile, please.

Luke Evans is an artist and photograper who works between London and his hometown of Hereford. Future exhibitions include *New Order III: British Art Today* at the Saatchi Gallery and *Contemporary Printmaking* at the RCA.

Ernst Fischer studied art in New York and Zurich, and filmmaking in London. He likes taking pictures of very large and very small things. He conceived of and built the microphotography rig he used for the shoot in this issue. He lives and works in New York City.

Julian Ganio is fashion editor at *Fantastic Man* and lives in London with his partner Brian Clivaz, of L'Escargot in Soho, and their three dogs, Jack Russells Mouse and Bear, and Doris the Bulldog.

Adrianna Glaviano is a freelance photographer who works on commissioned and personal projects. Born and raised in New York City, after studying she moved to Milan to work as a photographic assistant, and is now based in Paris.

Julia Grassi is a London-based photographer. Born and raised in Marseille, Julia works between Europe and Japan. She has contributed to titles including *Inventory Magazine*, *The Plant*, *The Green Soccer Journal*, *Kinfolk*, *The Weekender* and *Madame Figaro Japan*.

Klaus Haapaniemi is a Finnish-born artist, designer and restaurant critic. His work is influenced by pagan mysticism, nature, Finnish folklore, fantasy and the decorative arts. Klaus launched his own textile and design company in London in 2010.

Ben Houston is a dealer in antiquarian and rare books for the London-based firm Peter Harrington. He is an enthusiastic cocktail drinker and an unrepentant slow eater.

Kyle Hugall is an English writer who lives in New York City. He wears expensive pyjamas and hunts his food with hawks.

Jean Jullien is a French graphic designer now living in New York. His practice ranges from illustration, photography and video to costumes, installations, books, posters and clothing. In 2011 he founded Jullien Brothers. In 2012 he created News of the Times with Yann and Gwendal Le Bec.

Takamasa Kikuchi is an architect and writer based in London. His growing interests in Japanese food, culture and handicrafts have led him to explore his native Japan. He has contributed articles to publications including *Inventory Magazine* and *Kinfolk*.

Scarlett Kilcooley-O'Halloran is a born-and-bred Londoner who is now news editor at Vogue.co.uk. Outside of work she is a guest lecturer at the V&A, where she also runs workshops. She enjoys travelling, art and thrifting through markets.

Carl Kleiner is a Swedish image-maker who produces still lifes and portraits for fashion and lifestyle brands. He also directs moving-image work. He lives in Stockholm with his wife and two sons.

Tim Lahan is a graphic artist living and working in New York City. He failed his drawing class in high school, and gym class, twice.

Kelly MacLean is an American humourist and comedienne. Her work has been featured in *Reader's Digest* and *Los Angeles Magazine*, and she is best known for her blog on The Huffington Post.

Benjamin McMahon is a photographer from Yorkshire living in London and making pictures wherever he's sent for British *Vogue*, French *Vanity Fair*, American *Elle* and other nice folk like *The Gourmand*.

Antto Melasniemi is a Finnish chef who runs three restaurants in Helsinki, and has done pop-ups in London, Stockholm, Milan, Bangkok and Paris. He finds inspiration in shamanistic drinking and dancing.

Peta O'Brien is a food stylist, organic model maker, curator and art collector living and working in London. Responding to challenging briefs with an absolutist approach is just part of her daily life.

Ananda Pellerin is a London-based writer and editor. She writes for titles including AnOthermag.com, *Dazed*, *Time Out*, Postmatter.com and *Riposte*. She is the editor of *The Gourmand*, and the series editor of Penguin Press's *Philosophy in Transit* books.

Jo Ratcliffe is a London-based artist known for her kaleidoscopic animations, strange hand-drawn characters and spindly scenes, sometimes overlaid on live-action footage. Her previous clients include *Vogue*, Louis Vuitton, Lady Gaga, Kenzo, Barneys New York and Jimmy Choo.

Lisa Rovner is a storyteller. Through her work in film, photography, performance and the written word, she reflects a clear engagement with historical precedents and predecessors, and a desire to confront history with her story. She lives in London.

Bronia Stewart is a London-based photographer. She has exhibited in London and Mexico, and her work has featured in *The New Yorker*, *The Guardian*, *The Sunday Times*, *AnOther Magazine* and *Dazed* and on It's Nice That.

Yann Stofer lives and works in Paris, but his heart belongs to his hometown Bordeaux, where he enjoyed playing hardcore and drinking wine. His photographs possess a great deal of kindness, and primarily document his life and relationships with a realistic eye.

Gemma Tickle is a set designer living and working in London. She has collaborated on advertising, editorial and event-based projects for clients such as British *Vogue*, *Under the Influence*, Kate Spade and Nike.

Aaron Tilley is a still-life photographer based in east London. His graphic and conceptual style attracts a variety of British and international clients including *Elle*, *GQ*, *Kinfolk*, *The Guardian Weekend*, Google and Adidas.

Kingston Trinder is an aspirant writer and creative from New Zealand. He's also enamoured with the processes of commercial ideation, innovation and creation. That, and gazpacho. Expect his second book upon discounted shelves, ever so soon.

Tom Viney is a producer, filmmaker and writer. His next film, a co-production with the BBC, provisionally titled *The R&B Feeling*, broadcasts in spring 2015. It's full of screaming and nudity.

R.E.V
by
rêve en vert

SUSTAINABLE STYLE

Editor's Note

In this, our sixth issue, we wander hither and yon. There are Ernst Fischer's photos of roe, taken with his custom-built camera, in which the delicate becomes monumental. There is the dedication to delight of Jason Evans's 'Hungry Thirsty Happy Snappy': ten years of food from his website, The Daily Nice. Sam Bompas explores the relationship between drinking and the human body. And Lisa Rovner presents us with moments of great intimacy, as fruit is shared between two lovers' lips. Each of these contributors have sought and found a particular means of sharing their passions and their craft; we are delighted they have chosen to share it with us.

And as it is for them, *The Gourmand* has also striven to develop a more personal means of expression. In our case, it is the result of a collaboration with Monotype, one of the original metal-type foundries. Like recipes and preparations, our new, unique typeface, Gourmand Grotesque, is the result of generational refinement. With the folk at Monotype, we lifted letterforms from the shadows, and with craft and care developed a distinctive alphabet without losing the typeface's historical idiosyncrasies. In particular, there is the ampersand. It was discovered on a sheet marked "Do Not Use". We thought it was rather beautiful. So we're using it.

Beautiful too are the memories shared by Louise Benson, from the flickering flames of a Marylebone fire to the art on the walls of her grandparents' restaurant, the legendary Odin's. Modena-based chef Massimo Bottura, quite apart from running his three-star Michelin restaurant, Osteria Francescana, has been known to ask his protégés what they know of Russian Constructivism, helping them see beyond the day-to-day—affirming a connection between the arts, culinary or otherwise.

With this issue we also take a step into the interior to present a brief history of the home kitchen. In it, we tell how reformers gave way to modernists, and how three women would prove to have the greatest impact on how our cooking and dining spaces are organised today. And we look back on entertainer Liberace's deep wells of culinary generosity. His breakfast of baked eggs and parmesan was invariably eaten in the afternoon, and Kingston Trinder's touching essay glimmers in the shadow of the showman's signature candelabrum.

Yet more awaits. We are delighted to welcome Kelly MacLean, a comedienne, writer, actress and Huffington Post regular, who has been made giddy by the possibilities of veganism. Tom Viney talks to Jonathan Meades about places, people, food and his writing—in which it has been observed that his characters seem mostly to eat the sort of food that inspired Scarlett Kilcooley-O'Halloran's 'Fashion, with a Side of Fries'. Meanwhile the utterly indefinable Kyle Hugall strides through issue five with a flask in his pocket and a hawk on his arm.

But it is to Neneh Cherry's conversation with Clare Considine that we might draw your final attention. As a citizen of the world, now back in London, food has become a point of reference for the incomparable singer–songwriter, irrespective of setting. "Food represents harmony", she tells us. "It's about exploring my senses, relaxing, tuning in; I always feel like I want be wholly present, and food makes me present." There could be no more beautiful sentiment, nor any point better at which to wish you, dear reader, a safe journey through issue five.

Contents

12–15

16–19

20–27

28–31

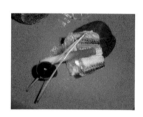

32–33

34–39

40–47

48–53

54–59

60–65

CONTENTS

66–73

74–81

82–89

90–97

98–103

104–111

112–113

114

115–118

120

Drinking has been the foremost leisure occupation across many cultures for millennia. Over the years this interest has led to elaborate rituals and arcane methodologies of intoxication. Many of our favourite—and all of the most disgusting—involve the body.

Body Shots

Rehabilitating Nature's Drinking Vessel

Words: Sam Bompas
Photography: Luke Evans

Bodily drinking techniques generate a sense of occasion, help people reach previously unachievable highs or a rapid drunk, or even provide a frisson of sensuality. First we'll explore how various regions of the body can be used for alcohol absorption, and then we'll consider how the body itself can be used as a drinking vessel.

At Bompas & Parr we first came across the notion that you could use any of the body's mucus membranes to ingest alcohol with our project Alcoholic Architecture. For this we generated a walk-in cloud of gin and tonic that intoxicated through the lungs as visitors inhaled. Respiratory scientists from CASE (the Centre for Altitude, Space and Extreme Environment Medicine) were our mixologists, calculating the ratio of spirit to mixer (a respectable 1:3) that visitors could safely breathe (responsibly).

Over the course of 40 minutes in the G&T mist, visitors absorbed the equivalent of a large UK standard measure across their respiratory epithelium. The high humidity also had the advantage of bringing out the botanicals in the gin, which could then be effectively paired with a drink in hand, for gustatory pleasure. While working with the scientists we further discovered that visitors would also be intoxicated through their eyeballs, a fact that prompted us to research the full array of options for alternative bodily intoxication. Some were far from pleasant.

BALL, SLAM, CHUG

First there's eyeballing, the absurd technique of ingesting vodka through one's eye socket. This form of consumption is said to have originated in the 2000s, potentially popularised by the film *Kevin & Perry Go Large*. It is a remarkably painful thing to do.

Fox News reported in 2010: "Hundreds of online videos that originated in the UK show teens pouring vodka directly into their eyes, straight from the bottle. The videos are getting hundreds of thousands of hits."

A man interviewed by police reported the experience to be like "a baseball bat hitting you in the back of the head—for about two to three minutes". And this seems timid in comparison to the wave of 'tammy slamming' said to have hit the States.

Tammy slamming is the practice of inserting a vodka-soaked tampon into the anus or vagina. According to The Huffington Post: "alcohol is absorbed directly into the bloodstream through the membrane walls", delivering an almost instantaneous rush. KPHO News in Phoenix reports that there have been some cases of alcohol poisoning from these methods. In addition to using tampons, the broadcaster claims that teens are taking part in "butt chugging", where alcohol is consumed rectally with a tube or hose. The Huffington

Post posits: "Butt chugging seems to be done to avoid having alcohol breath."

As it's difficult to calculate the number of practitioners, save for a few cases of hospitalisation, we suspect the considerable media coverage is due to mild hysteria around the practice, and the titillation factor associated with the ages and orifices involved.

What's more, neither tammy slamming nor butt chugging are likely to help practitioners avoid alcohol breath. This comes from alcohol in the blood leaving the body through the lungs as you exhale, and does not originate in the stomach. Butt chuggers also miss out on savouring the taste of alcohol.

SKULLDUGGERY

Perhaps more rewarding is the use of bodies as vessels to drink from. The first known drinking vessel made from a human skull was found in Gough's Cave in Somerset—dated by archaeologists to 12,700 BC— a time of mystic druidical rites. But skull cups have been used throughout history, and Vikings were said to have toasted their victories with the skulls of their defeated enemies. Recently, the Japanese have developed an arguably more upbeat (and more erotic) bodily drinking ritual in the form of 'wakame sake'. This consists of drinking alcohol from a woman's body (though it is easy to imagine a male counterpart), and, according to one connoisseur, here's how it's done: "The woman closes her legs tight enough that the triangle between the thighs and mons pubis form a cup, and then pours sake down her chest into this triangle. Her partner then drinks the sake from there. The name comes from the idea that the woman's pubic hair in the sake resembles soft seaweed (wakame) floating in the sea." It really is quite poetic.

More harrowing perhaps is the rumour, which we've not been able to substantiate, about the mysterious Japanese gay bar where the drinks are mixed in the bus boys' anuses. The server then squats over the cocktail glass, excreting a slurry of the mixed drink to be enjoyed by customers of refined tastes. When we visited Japan it was impossible to track down such a bar, despite many involved conversations with hotel concierges. Miming only confused the matter.

SYMPHONY OF MOIST JOY

Develop your own bodily drinking ritual with this cocktail by "The Only William". See if you can come up with a new celebratory practice that rehabilitates the body shot. For the Symphony of Moist Joy recipe → p115.

Groundcherry Kiss

A film by Lisa Rovner

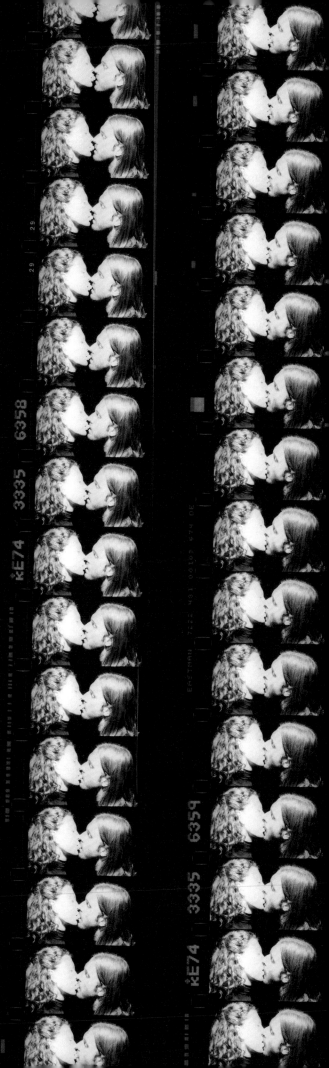

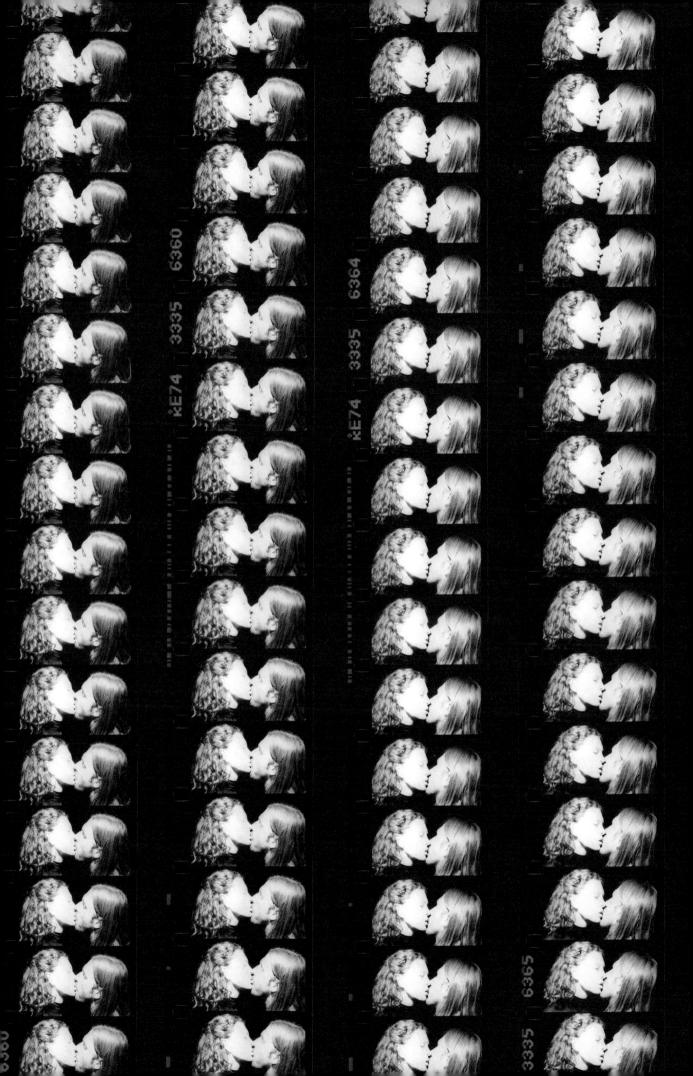

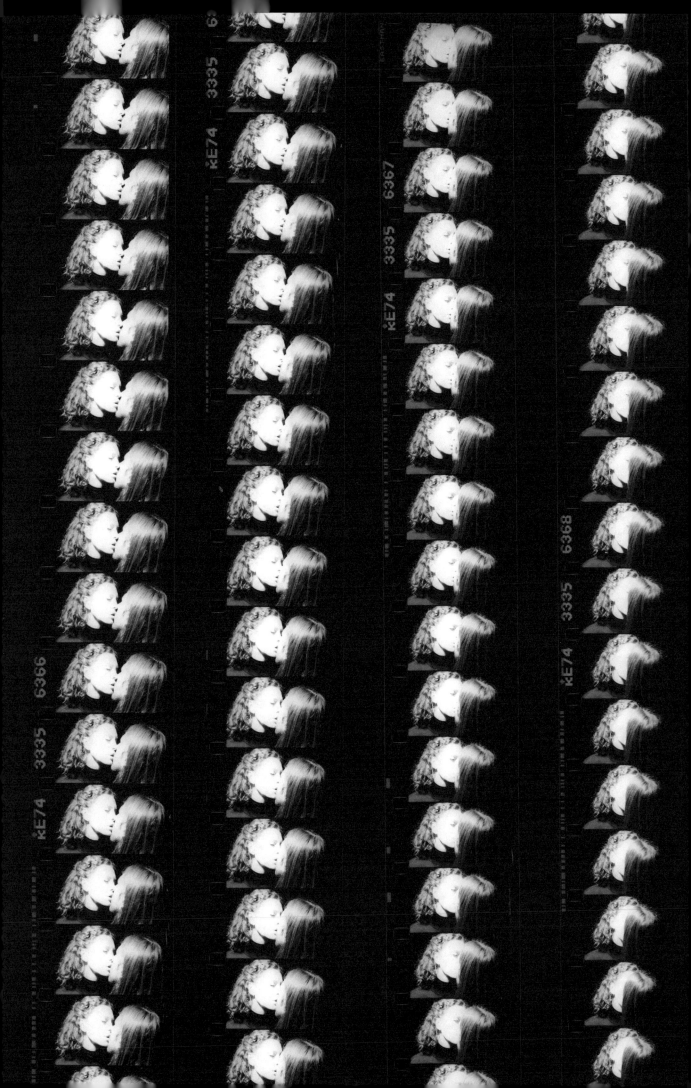

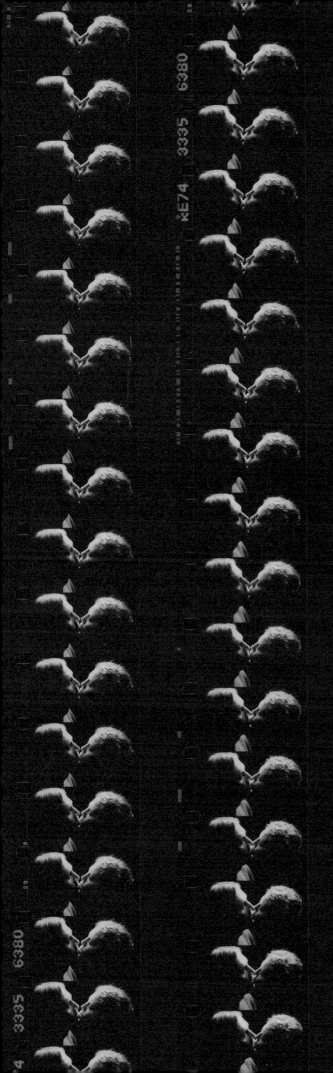

The idea for how we'd shoot the kiss came to me as I remembered *Funeral Parade of Roses*, a Japanese film by Toshio Matsumoto set in 1960s gay countercultural Tokyo. There's one scene where it's just a couple kissing —I'd seen it years ago and it really stuck with me. I loved the camera work, the camera as witness. I also loved working within the constraints of 16mm film. We only had 11 minutes to play with, only 11 minutes to get it right. No special effects here. It just is what it is.

Going in, I thought the film would be about the execution of a simple idea. But in reality the feeling of the kiss overwhelms the rigidity of the concept. The fruit is called a physalis, or ground-cherry. We got it at New Covent Garden Market in south London, which is open from midnight until early morning. I'd never been before and I thought it was going to be this beautiful place, but it's industrial-sized, unadorned and full of machine noise. And those traders do not like to haggle.

Groundcherry Kiss was also influenced by Andy Warhol's 50-minute film *Kiss*. Obviously that was much more radical at the time because there were men kissing men, and white and black people kissing. It was a wholly different concept, but it was a strong visual reference for me nonetheless. Warhol once said, "Everyone ends up kissing the wrong person goodnight." In this case it's just the opposite. Of course our filmic kiss was staged, but it's a real couple and there's no denying

the intensity between them. The couple have been together for four years and married for two of those. As a viewer you become almost a voyeur to their intimacy. It was quite a surprise, re-watching it, to see a realness that is so often difficult to capture.

Director: Lisa Rovner • Director of Photography: Jeremy Valender • Hair & Makeup: Ruth Coutinho
Gaffer: Grzegorz Krzeszowiec • Models: Sion & Tiffany Phillips • Production: Gelardin Management
Creative Direction: *The Gourmand*
Watch *Groundcherry Kiss* at gourmand.co.uk

Words: Marina Tweed
Photography: Benjamin McMahon

Of Lived in Beauty

Kettle's Yard

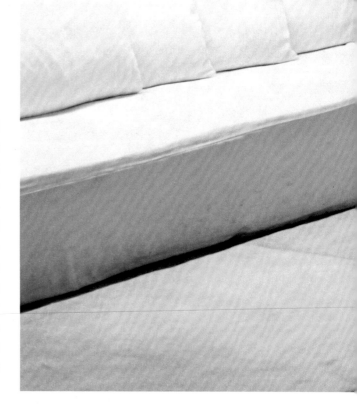

Jim Ede, collector and curator and friend to artists, is considered one of Britain's most influential figures in the development of people's appreciation of contemporary art in Britain. His understanding of the relationship between shape and form, as well as the importance of composition, balance and light, brought Ede to establish his house-gallery, Kettle's Yard, in Cambridge in the 1950s. It was not only a residence for him and his wife, Helen, it was also a home for his beloved collection. To this day, the property stands as a testament to this extraordinary man.

In 1956, Jim Ede wrote to artist and friend David Jones: "It would be interesting to be lent a great house on the verge of a city—or a place of beauty in a town (Cambridge I have in mind) and make it all that I could of lived in beauty, each room an atmosphere of quiet and simple charm, and open to the public... and for such a living creation I would give all that I have in pictures and lovely objects." A year later, Jim and Helen opened Kettle's Yard, a cottage that had fallen into disrepair and which was to become their carefully curated home, and one that welcomed the public and, in particular, students of Cambridge University. Kettle's Yard was not established to be a

1.

Ede befriended painters Ben and Winifred Nicholson, who were husband and wife, during his time at the Tate Gallery. With Ben's work not enjoying commercial success, the artist happily sold paintings to Ede for the cost of the canvas and the frame. Over time, Ede collected approximately 50 of Ben's works.

Ben was especially interested in painting still lifes, and Ede particularly admired his ability to translate a "continuity from [his works] into the everyday world of the twenties and thirties". Works such as *Apples and Pears* (fig. 1), with its simple subject matter, composition and colour, was a source of inspiration for Ede's vision at Kettle's Yard.

typical museum or a gallery. It was a space where the couple could share their appreciation of contemporary art and objects in a domestic setting. Ede encouraged daily open houses, inviting students for tea and conversation.

Ede was assistant curator at the Tate Gallery from 1921 to 1936, and through his work encountered many artists—including Picasso, Chagall and Miró—many of whom became great friends of his. He had a strong notion of which pieces might be exciting to future generations, making him, in effect, the Tate's first curator of contemporary art.

2.

In 1931, Ben and Winifred's marriage came to an end, though Winifred remained a close friend of Ede's. He admired the pride she took in bringing a "woman's attitude" to her work, and acquired her painting *Cyclamen and Primula* (fig. 2). It was one of several she had painted in Switzerland in the early 1920s, and she described the series as "sunlight in white paper". She continues: "Ben had given me a pot of lilies of the valley—mughetti—in a tissue paper wrapper—this I stood on the windowsill—behind was the azure blue, mountain, lake, sky, all there— and the tissue paper wrapper held the secret of the

3.

Religion was important to Ede, and his close friend the artist David Jones was also a believer. A veteran of World War II, Jones had been greatly affected by his experiences in the trenches, and he eventually found solace in the Roman Catholic Church. Jones's faith comes through in his work *Flora in Calix Light* (fig. 4), which shows a goblet, a reference to the Eucharistic chalice, and intricate plants and flowers sprout from within—a fusion of the daily with the divine.

Ede's humble salary meant that many of the pieces at Kettle's Yard were acquired through exchange or given out of generosity by his artist-friends. Many were everyday objects that embodied the simple

universe. That picture painted itself, and after that the same theme painted itself on that windowsill, in cyclamen, primula or cineraria—sunlight on leaves, and sunlight shining transparent through lens and through the mystery of tissue paper... I have often wished for another painting spell like that, but never had one."

In the sitting room of the cottage is a wooden cider-press screw, detached from its original frame, the spiral structure forming a refined table. Resting on this are two elegant crystal decanters, and at the peak of this tableau hangs Joan Miró's *Tic Tic* (fig. 3). In the bottom left corner of the painting is a small yellow circle.

4.

pleasure he found when looking at shape and form: a door knocker, a spiral of stones, a pair of jelly moulds. Plants and books are arranged amongst vessels, glassware and goblets, a grouping of the latter described by Ede as "being like a golden city". Sculpture and pottery complement each room at Kettle's Yard, and Ede was especially fond of his collection of bowls by Austrian-born studio potter Lucie Rie, whose work is in line with his own appreciation for simple shapes, and which are now highly collectable.

Ede would point to this when he was instructing undergraduates in the importance of balance: "If I put my finger over the spot at the top right all the rest of the picture slid into the left-hand bottom corner. If I covered the one at the bottom, horizontal lines appeared, and if somehow I could take out the tiny red spot in the middle everything flew to the edges."

To the side of the cider press sits a pewter bowl on a low wooden chest. Inside the bowl is a lemon. Ede would remove the lemon—as he had 'removed' the yellow dot of the painting—instructing the students to see how the composition of the whole room would change. "This gave me a much needed chance to mention God, by saying that if I had another name for God, I think it would be balance."

Gradually, Ede grew disenchanted by the uphill struggle to highlight the relevance of contemporary art at the Tate Gallery and beyond, and in 1936 he and Helen left England. Over the next 20 years they lived abroad, residing in Morocco and France and regularly visiting the United States. During this time he concentrated on lecturing and writing, continuing to expand his collection all the while. It was in Morocco that two candlesticks (fig. 5) caught his eye. Though paired together at Kettle's Yard, they were in fact purchased some hundred miles apart. With the natural light at the house greatly affecting the composition of each room, the house offers different experiences at various times of day, or when lit by candlelight in the evening.

After living abroad for 20 years, Ede and his wife returned to England to be closer to their children. It was then that they settled on the four derelict cottages of Kettle's Yard. Local architect Roland Aldridge worked with Ede to restore the buildings, and in 1957 Jim and Helen moved in. In 1966, Ede bequeathed Kettle's Yard and its entire collection to Cambridge University, though he remained its resident and honorary curator until 1973 when, due to Helen's poor health and the increasing difficulty of daily upkeep at the house, the couple relocated to Helen's hometown, Edinburgh. In 1970 and 1971, extensions were added to the Kettle's Yard site, including a contemporary exhibition space—a design by Leslie Martin that contrasted with the original cottages. After his departure, Ede remained in close contact with the team at Kettle's Yard, and, though he died in 1990 his daily routine is upheld, with the house still welcoming visitors daily.

5.

In memory of Michael Harrison (30th April 1947 to 25th April 2013), director of Kettle's Yard 1992–2011, who rescued and expanded Jim Ede's vision to create the international centre for the visual arts that it is today.

FASHION, WITH A SIDE OF FRIES

Words: Scarlett Kilcooley-O'Halloran
Photography: Aaron Tilley • Set Design: Gemma Tickle

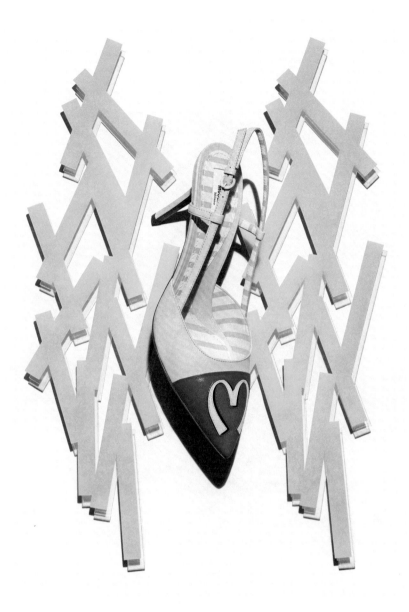

Leather Slingback shoe
by Moschino

Fashion and food. For many people they don't seem like easy bedfellows. But as recent catwalk outings have shown, the two are enjoying a well-documented affair. From Chanel's Shopping Centre and Anya Hindmarch's collaboration with Kellogg's to Jeremy Scott's McDonald's Moschino makeover, fashion designers are finding perverse pleasure in mixing the high and the low, the upmarket and the mass produced.

A wonderful feeling of familiarity accompanied Hindmarch's Bourbon-biscuit bag, Coco Pops clutch and Frosties tote as they were walked down her AW14 runway. The grrrr-eat grin of Tony the Tiger took us back to hurried school mornings, the gleeful 'Eeny, meeny, miny, moe' ritual of the cereal variety pack, the soggy consistency if you didn't eat with speed, and the acquired taste of toothpaste mingling with the bits in your back teeth as you ran out the door. Same too for Karl Lagerfeld's Chanel supermarket aisles, set up inside Paris's Grand Palais, and Charlotte Olympia's Chinese takeaway-box bags. They're fun, imaginative and comforting in a way that only the everyday can be.

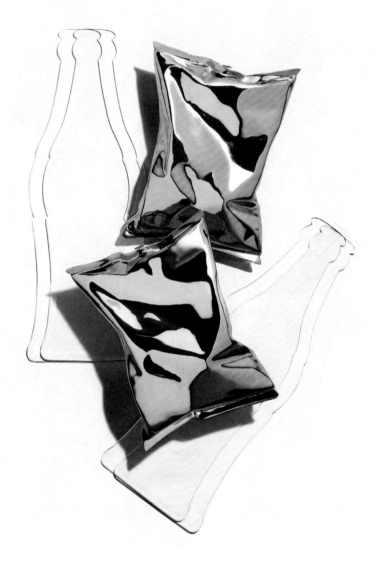

Crisp Packet, metal in green clutch
by Anya Hindmarch

But is it all an attention-grabbing gimmick that has a one-season sell-by-date? Yes and no. Food references have always been on the menu de la mode. Lulu Guinness's limited-edition Chocolate Box bag made it onto the arms of the sartorially savvy at the turn of this century, and Juergen Teller's "Start Me Up" shoot for the May 2003 issue of British *Vogue* featured Kate Moss wearing a long-sleeved banana top that stylist Bay Garnett had found in a thrift store, and which sparked Phoebe Philo's vision for Chloé SS04. Jeremy Scott first mooted his interpretation of consumerism with

a Snickers sweater in 2006, and the Dolce & Gabbana boys regularly call on the fruits of their native Sicily to play out their odes to the Mediterranean isle, most recently the zesty lemons, courgettes and pomegranates of SS12.

So why are food fashion crossovers hitting the headlines now more than ever? Back to Scott for that one. Unlike an inoffensive banana or a pretty box of chocolates, he took the theme to new heights (or depths) when he served up his McDonald's-inspired collection for Moschino in February 2014.

Imperial Corn Flakes and Frosties, multi-printed snake clutch
by Anya Hindmarch

He couldn't have chosen a more recognised or divisive logo if he'd tried, and it struck a chord.

Fast food on the runway highlights the parallels between the conveyor-belt speed of the fashion industry and the fuel-on-demand nature of Maccy D's. The power to command column inches has been undeniable, as has the Moschino collection's commercial success. It is precisely this level of exposure that gives fashion's food fixation a shelf life.

Incorporating familiar symbols of consumerism and showing them in a new light is something straight from Warhol's songbook (Scott and Hindmarch have abandoned food for Barbie and school stickers, respectively, for SS15, although the message remains the same). But perhaps the reason we keep seeing a return to all things edible is because it does the job so well. There is no better way to get a universal message across than with something we can all relate to, even if it is a one-season-at-a-time fling.

For Jackson Berg's Peanut Butter Parfait with Toasted Frosties, and Simon Gregory's Cornflake Tart recipes → p117

The Hunter, the Hunted and Me

Words: Kyle Hugall
Illustration: Jean Jullien

Hunting game is one thing—sloe gin coursing through your veins, a 12-bore Holland & Holland unleashing a murderous barrage on anything with wings and a pulse. But hunting game with hawks is something else entirely.

Any old ruddy, gout-riddled lord of the manor can bag brace after brace of feathery friends on a decent drive once the Glorious Twelfth rolls around. You don't need vast amounts of skill. You don't even need to be sober. But falconry involves a mystical combination of know-ledge, intuition and luck, as well as a deep connection with both the land and your accipitrine consort. When you take guns out of the equation and pit nature against nature, the odds are evened. It's a fairer fight where any-thing can happen.

The art of falconry is a truly ancient pursuit that began in Mesopotamia over 4,000 years ago. It spread to Europe around AD 400, where it quickly became a sport of kings, who collected birds of prey like Saddam Hussein collected gold-plated AK-47s. In the 900-year-old Bayeux Tapestry, King Harold can be found bossing it out on horseback with his trusty hawk perched on his arm. Falconry was practised mainly by the aristocracy, and species were allocated in relation to social rank. Earls hunted with per-egrine falcons, knights with saker falcons and so on. (My own baronial status requires that I hunt with a Harris hawk —a lethal pack hunter that's as beautiful as it is deadly.)

The relationship between the falconer and the raptor is deeply spiritual, and bonding with your hawk is crucial if you're going to have any success filling your larder with game. During the pre-hunt bonding process there comes a moment when eye contact is made and you stare deep into each other's souls. The hawk's intense, inquisitive stare demands respect. It's a fine balance between feeling like you're falling in love and feeling like you're about to have your tongue ripped out of your head by the sharpest beak you've ever seen. Once connected you become family, working together to hunt your quarry, which could be any-thing from rabbit or hare to grouse, pheasant or even deer.

The invention of gunpowder quickly rendered falconry nearly obsolete, when guns replaced birds as more reli-able and effective methods of hunting. Today falconry remains a pretty obscure pastime, eclipsed by depressing-ly lame pursuits like golf.

But its historical importance is unquestionable. And it's hard to put into words just how epic it feels to stride into the wilderness in good boots and a deerstalker, with a fe-rocious bird of prey perched on your glove like you're some kind of deranged medieval king. Hunting with hawks not only connects you to the land and nature in profound ways, it also connects you to something ancient, almost primal: a 4,000-year-old bond between man and bird that can be described in no other way but pure magic.

For James Lowe's Grouse, Bread Sauce and Pickled Mulberries recipe → p116

Hungry Thirsty Happy Snappy

Words ⊠ Photography: Jason Evans

In 2001 the Japanese cosmetics giant Shiseido sent me on a two-month, round-the-world trip. I was to photograph whatever I found beautiful and email the results back to their Paris gallery, where the show would grow, day by day. The kit for the project was big and heavy, and the technology was largely unsupported in Africa and Asia – though the equivalent would fit in your back pocket today. When the first cameraphone came out I did a similar project on a camping trip to New Zealand for Nick Knight's Showstudio. The image quality wasn't all that, but the ease of transmission was radical.

The technological developments at the beginning of the twenty-first century have been truly mind-boggling, and we invite them into our lives with barely a thought for how they will change our work, our relationships, ourselves. Can you remember what you did before smartphones? In less than seven years those devices have impacted on us in ways we have yet to fathom.

By 2004 the quality and affordability of digital cameras, plus easier access to and from the web, led me to think about a way to consolidate my own street-based snapshot work. I did not want to make a formal project. I enjoy photography as a verb: organic and responsive. I live through my eyes, a simple pleasure. Colours and patterns, light and shade, usually thrill me more than sophisticated cultural constructs. I want to share my enthusiasm, pointing to the joys that reward paying attention. The images that I post on The Daily Nice are, for me, positive affirmations, good news released into the world in opposition to our scaremongering media.

Every day for ten years I have posted a picture of something that made me happy, partly as a small act of resistance. The idea was for the minimal site to be something to take in along with your morning stretch and yawn – an antidote to what the *Daily Mail* et al. might have in store for you. Taking ownership of your happiness, your positive wellbeing, without having to validate that participation with a transaction, is vital. I have no advertising, and there is no online archive. When it's gone, it's gone. I prefer to enjoy and then let go, confident that there will always be something else to excite me if I keep my eyes open. These simple, effective ideas run counter to the 'bigger cages, longer chains' freedoms of neo-liberal society. Always carrying a dedicated Daily Nice camera is a physical reminder of the therapeutic chance for positivity.

Sustaining this simple format for so long is also an exercise in the power of limits. Initially the journey was triggered by sight, but gradually encompassed my other senses. Now, ten years on, The Daily Nice has evidenced the tactile and the smelly, the cosy and the harmonious.

In my line of work I get to travel. Blessed with a cast-iron stomach, and with my vegan days behind me, I've been an experience junky in the provisions market, at fancy tables and at the street vendor's pitch. Some of the resulting food porn is collected here, including language-barrier dietary decisions based on pointing and smiles. I'll never be sure what that was, but it was delicious.

For Jason Evans's Wholesome Kale Salad recipe → p115

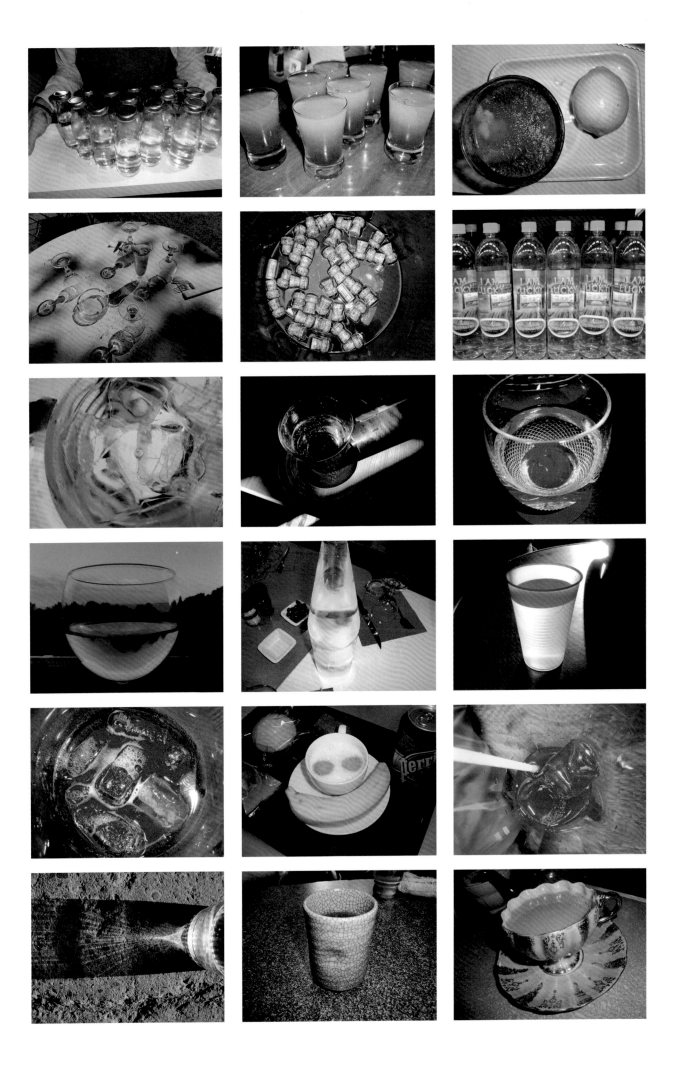

MASSIMO BOTTURA

RODCHENKO AND THE BEAUTY OF THE POTATO

Words: Ananda Pellerin
Photography: Adrianna Glaviano

At the helm of his Modena restaurant, Osteria Francescana, for nearly ten years, chef Massimo Bottura has delighted in applying a finely tuned conceptual bent to constructing dishes with layers of meaning, humour and sense of place. Tangential, kinetic and incapable of standing still for long, Bottura feeds his creativity with an ever-expanding interest in art (he and his wife Lara are avid collectors), music (he owns thousands of records) and philosophy (he speaks excitedly about Thomas Aquinas and Roland Barthes). Bottura is the first to say that his three-star Michelin success is not just down to him (he often refers to 'we', instead of 'I'). With the same core team at Francescana from the start, he doesn't just teach his staff technique but brings Russian Constructivism and other influences into the kitchen, sharing his ability to see beyond the confines of the day-to-day. His new, first-ever English-language book *Never Trust a Skinny Italian Chef* does have recipes, but it is more a grouping of stories, photos, influences and ideas from over his 25 years of professional cooking. Here, Bottura talks about the future of the chef, his plans for a culinary university and the importance of the potato.

THREE MICHELIN STARS

I decided to give up on the family business and not become a lawyer. My brothers pushed me to follow my passions—art, music and food—and I ended up picking food. My first restaurant was a little trattoria outside of Modena, and my father wasn't very happy, so I said, "You'll see, one day I'll have three stars." I decided to do it, to do my best, to create a team, because this is the most important thing. If you work by yourself you don't get anywhere. It's like soccer or any other team sport. Then, in November 2011, I received a phone call from Michelin and they told me we had three stars, and I cried. The dream of my life became a reality.

ABSENCE OF SIN

I'm a contemporary chef, living in contemporary times. This is a special moment—we want something that is real and intense. When you lose yourself in technique and in too much overthinking, you lose the sense of being a chef. A chef feeds the palate, first of all. After that, the mind and stomach. When you get up from my table you feel so light, your digestion is already done. We think about making things that are delicious, and having a long, beautiful tasting menu, but we don't want to load you up with calories, heavy fats, any kind of chemicals; we want to show that you can have a very enjoyable, poetic, sensational meal that's full of flavour. Even the desserts are very light. It doesn't have to be this sin or breaking the rules, or get you thinking, "I shouldn't have done that."

THE BURNT PAN

A while ago the team had a very deep conversation after our staff meal and someone asked me a question, and it opened up a Pandora's Box about Duchamp and Warhol. Most of them didn't know who Duchamp was, so I said, "OK, I'll give you 48 hours to find out about him and write a few pages." We are pushing them in an intellectual way, so it's not just about chopping, sautéing and cooking, it's about the ideas. Another time I said one of our dishes was based on Rodchenko, it was all shadows and grey, and they did their own research to find out more—one guy wrote four or five pages. They really take it seriously.

The future of the chef is not about the burnt pan, it's about culture. And that's why I push young chefs to study, not to rush to be in the kitchen. Finish high school—go to university. Just grow. That's impossible when you're 15—they should be studying everything: language, at least English, a little bit of French to travel, and they have to know about art, of course.

A POTATO WAITING TO BECOME A TRUFFLE

This is a dish that is a version of a baked potato. There's no particularly avant-garde technique going on here, you simply bend your mind to think of the potato as something beautiful. Tubers have saved nations, and killed nations, and people have moved because of potatoes.

It's not about fireworks or powders or things like that, but the idea itself. We've had diners come from Asia or America, all over, and Italians who are very sceptical about this "potato waiting to become a truffle". I remember one traveller from Hong Kong, his face was illuminated: he couldn't believe how good the potato was. He kept saying to me, "Thank you, I've never had potato that was so delicious in my entire life." And it broke down the whole barrier, it wasn't about whether it was a gourmet dish, it wasn't about whether there's truffle there, it's about eating something and you're so focused on the ingredient that you leave the table and you remember that ingredient. We put aside the ego of the chef, and we just use the technique to create a real truth on the plate.

MORE ON THE POTATO

You know, if you live your everyday life, would you eat potato or truffle? If I had to choose I would eat potato. To me a potato has to be a potato, and most of the time it's better than a truffle. Chefs don't have to get so deep into buying caviar, or blue lobster from Britain, or sea scallops, or whatever. If you express the potato, in the right way, with the perfect technique, with a great idea that comes from inside, you can get your three stars. It was very revolutionary for Michelin, because we're promoting these kinds of dishes with subversive elements. This is a revolutionary message!

TEARS AT THE TABLE

I've seen people crying at the table. There was a couple dining at Francescana, they were maybe 80 years old, and they were eating "compression of pasta and beans"; they were chewing the crust of parmigiano, and a couple of tears came out of the man's eye. I said, "What happened?" And he said, "When I chew this, I go back to my childhood." I was so touched. Or the Polish girl with her boyfriend who flew in from England to have dinner here, and the potato was the last dish, and she started crying, she couldn't stop. She said it reminded her of her grandmother's potato soufflé. Of course it wasn't the same thing, but it's the taste. I got so emotional—this is the best part of being a chef.

We feel very connected to someone like Michael Pollan, who tells people that nutrition is not mathematical, it's emotional—this is something we've always believed. We try to give meaning to everything we do. We don't have that many tables, and everyone who comes through is important.

NOT MY STATION

We want to make sure we don't get stuck in a way of cooking or a mannerism, so that's why we love having young chefs come in and we keep them on their toes, moving them around from pastry to first courses etc. No matter what, you have to keep it alive and keep it fresh and don't get caught up in the day-to-day. They have to move around. And they hate it. But they'll thank you one day.

I always say to young chefs, you have to travel a lot, and with your ears and eyes open. You learn the secret of the dumpling from a Chinese chef, and keep the things that you need to evolve your cuisine, your expression. But never forget your backpack, which contains where you come from and who you are. And in your backpack you have to have humility, passion and a dream.

GESTURE

Why do I have to know all these things about art? Why do I have all these ideas from jazz and things? Because these are my passions, and I'm living it all every day. It's not like tomorrow I'm going to the seaside to lie under the sun, I'm not doing that, I hate that. I can be under the sun but I can't stop thinking. Art is not what you see, art is making the invisible, visible. You catch the idea of art and you grow, you understand so many things. So culture brings responsibility, responsibility brings awareness, and awareness brings social gesture.

HOMETOWN, FORWARD

Modena is an old Italian town, and when people visit they aren't expecting to see the contemporary design and contemporary artwork that we have at Francescana. I am always influenced by the ingredients and cooking of Emilia-Romagna, but I'm also trying to create a national cuisine that is an expression of each territory, that is an expression of small realities close to the farm and the fishermen and cheesemakers—people who are giving us some of the most incredible ingredients in the world.

A recent project is that we've saved an agricultural school close to Modena because it was about to shut down, and now there's a waiting list. We introduced the idea of chefs going into the kitchen with their hands dirty with earth and smelling of milk, so they'll know how difficult it is to work the land and to milk the cows at four in the morning and make parmigiano every day. Also there's a beautiful eighteenth-century villa that is abandoned, so we're going to rebuild this place and give it life by establishing a culinary university. All of this reflects our process; we're always thinking about the next project and moving ourselves forward. If you don't go against gravity you're going to just go backwards. You have to keep pushing that envelope.

Home is Where the Cooking Happens

Neneh Cherry is back in London. The singer-songwriter says she cannot stand moving house. But she's been at it again. After an extended stint in Sweden, she and her husband, Cameron, and two of their daughters, Tyson and Mabel, have decided to return to Britain. Earlier this year, 50-year-old Neneh released *Blank Project*, her first solo album in 18 years. Born to a Swedish mother and father from Sierra Leone, Neneh was once a member of post-punk band The Slits, and notoriously performed her biggest global hit, "Buffalo Stance", on *Top of the Pops* when she was eight-months pregnant. A few years ago she also co-hosted cult-hit cooking show *Neneh and Andi Dish It Up,* on BBC Two.

Today we're sitting in Neneh's unassuming flat in Westbourne Grove, which is awaiting a truckload of boxes from Sweden and the idiosyncratic stamp that only your own stuff can bring. But despite the lack of trinkets, this place couldn't feel more like a home. 17-year-old Mabel arrives bearing gifts from the local Portuguese bakery; her boyfriend sits quietly with his guitar, listening contentedly as we chat; friends roll in and put the kettle on,

Neneh is in a nostalgic mood. She chats with energy about her mother, Moki, who died in 2009. Neneh grew up all over the world—from the Swedish woods to northern Italy, leafy Vermont to the Chelsea Hotel. Her mother brought a small transportable kitchen with them everywhere the family went. The idea was simple: home is where the cooking happens. We settle down to discuss music, being on the move and how food has played a part in Neneh's life at each and every turn.

Tell me about your childhood in Sweden.
I grew up with my stepfather [jazz musician Don Cherry]. He had come to Sweden with Sonny Rollins and met my mother, who was an artist. A lot of jazz musicians during that era ended up staying in Europe because America was too segregated. The sound of free jazz and that positive anger, it freed them. In their music they were experiencing limitless possibilities, and then they'd go back into everyday life, and the reality was something they couldn't break out of. So musicians and artists came and stayed in Stockholm and they went to Paris and Rome. These places became creative hubs.

Why did your family move out of Stockholm?
My parents had pretty big ideas about wanting to change things in society, and giving me and my brother [Eagle Eye Cherry] an insight into how big the world was, how to be part of a greener planet. We moved into this schoolhouse an hour and a half north of Malmö. My grandfather was from this area of Sweden, and my mother used to describe it as a kind of 'nowhere'. It's in the woods and there's something magical about it.
    My mother painted the whole house in different colours. It was September when we moved in and there was heather everywhere. One room was all purple with dark-green skirting boards, one was green and one was yellow. It was an amazing creation.

What was the day-to-day like there?
It's funny because you listen to my stepdad in interviews and he always talks about the house. Chopping wood and growing food and all of that stuff. But the reality was my mother did most of it. He played a lot of music!
    At the time, I fantasised about living in an Ikea catalogue. I wanted to have the life that all of my friends had. When I was hanging out with them I used to pray that I would get fed by their parents. I loved the normality. My mother cooked with Indian spices, and we ate pretty exotic food. But for me, what I was eating at other households was exotic. The bland stuff was the stuff to die for.
    My house was vegetarian for a pretty long time, but we didn't stay that way. I can remember the day when my mum decided to cook a chicken, and our vegetarian friends turned up. I was screaming out the window: "We're gonna have chickeeeeeeen!"

What was it like living in New York?
We lived for a while at the Chelsea Hotel. One of the women who cleaned on our floor used to have a hotplate in the closet where they kept all the linen, which was also their little tea-break corner. She used to fry steak, and I would go in and sit with her and she'd make me a steak sandwich. That smell coming down the hallway, I used to follow it like a *Dawn of the Dead* zombie.
    I remember my mum cooking in the hotel room. There was this one time when some record-company people came to talk to my stepdad. She made pasta. And she was in the bathroom draining the pasta down the toilet without a strainer. Some of it fell in and she just took it out and washed it and served it. I don't think she liked our guests very much.

Your mother sounds like a real matriarch.
She affected a lot of people, but her art suffered.
She was a bit broken-hearted because she put in all
of this energy and never quite reaped the rewards
of creative release, recognition, or a place that she
could really claim for herself. I think that can happen
to a lot of women when they're making a family.

But anyone that knew her felt the power of her
creativity. It was in everything—it was in the way that
we lived, the way our house looked, the way that she
cooked, the way that she made the garden and the
love that she did it all with. And I think that, for her,
was also her art. That's why she gave it so much time
and love. It wasn't just that life stole her away. She
would say things like, "I'm a fiend for love; I'm a fiend

**When you were 14 you moved to London on your
own. What was that like?**
I met Andrea [her best friend and *Dish It Up* co-host]
pretty early on. Cooking was a really big part of our
friendship. It was like, "put the music on, let's cook".
Andrea and I felt that we could share a place cultur-
ally with food. Sundays for both of us always had
a soundtrack: Dinah Washington, Bessie Smith,
Johnny Guitar Watson and Stevie Wonder; we'd cook
chicken, drinking hot toddies and dancing to Earth,
Wind & Fire. I'm still an absolute sucker for food that
has soul. I don't care where it comes from. I don't
mean specifically sweet potato pie, chicken and black-
eyed beans, or rice and peas. I'm talking about food
from the heart. Fine dining is, of course, amazing fun,

Food seems to be linked to a lot of your memories. Do you have one meal that stands out for you?

I have a meal that comes to mind at the weirdest moments—sometimes just before I fall asleep. We were staying in Turin, in northern Italy. Me and my mother went to lunch. The tablecloths were starched and white. It was very quiet in the restaurant—almost eerie but in a nice way. Like how it sounds in the restaurant in *The Godfather* just before Al Pacino goes and gets the gun from behind the loo, but less heavy. There was this smell of Parmesan and minestrone in the air. And then the dish of the day was brought to the table. It was a stewed lamb thing that came in a beautiful white bowl on a beautiful white plate. It was soft. It was almost sensual.

It was very clean and very deep, and it's a food memory that has its own space for me. The deep throwback of that taste is almost like a mantra.

Do you think food and music always share a connection for you?

I like music that creates a beautiful atmosphere. I listen to jazz when I'm cooking for that reason. I also listen to reggae, Brazilian and Cuban music —when you listen to it, you can almost smell it. To me, food represents harmony. It's about exploring my senses, relaxing, tuning in; I always feel like I want be wholly present, and food makes me present.

For Mabel's Beet and Dark Chocolate Cake recipe → p117

Jonathan Meades

The Terminator

Words: Tom Viney
Photography: Yann Stofer

Jonathan Meades lives in Marseille. He is primarily a writer, and over the years has gained a reputation as a singular voice in architecture, topography, culture and place. He has also seen a full and accomplished broadcast career, with over 50 documentaries under his belt. This is to say nothing of his sunglasses, almost never off, which probably deserve a career of their own. In another life Meades was the restaurant critic for *The Times*, though he happily gave up journalism years ago, and continues to write—most recently his autobiography, *An Encyclopaedia of Myself*—and make programmes on subjects that still hold his interest. Meades is also something of an oddity, in a broader sense. In stark contrast to the often-plodding pace of British television, his programmes are equal parts Auntie-says formality and cheese-dream surrealist. In 1997, to introduce *Remember the Future*, a programme on the architecture and future-fetishism of Britain in the post-war period, he famously recreated the opening scene of *The Terminator*, casting himself in the lead role: crouching naked in a ball and bathed in CGI lightning. We met with Meades to discuss, among other things, Chinese food, France, British gastronomic culture and, somewhere along the line, Greg Wallace.

I know that you hate food. But I'd like to ask you a couple of questions about your experiences with it nonetheless.

Well, I don't hate food. I dislike most writing about it. And I don't think writing about it has much improved since it's become such a fashion item, which happened in the last quarter-century or so. I got into it completely by chance. I had written throughout my twenties, mostly on literary subjects and television. I wrote a book of short stories, and, as a result, people kept asking me to do various bits of journalism. Initially I was quite enthusiastic, I thought it would be interesting to write about food for a few months. But a few months turned into 15 years.

There were various problems. If you're doing something weekly, you get identified with that subject—whatever else you do seems cursory. On the other hand, every time I said I was going to leave they threw more money at me, which made the situation even worse. *The Times* thought they were getting someone who would do a comic turn, they were rather astonished to discover that I actually knew quite a lot about food, and was interested in it as something other than a vehicle for making gags. So it rather changed the complexion of how food writing was done at that point—I'm talking about the mid-1980s. It had been either people doing gags or doing very factual stuff. I did both. For the first five or six years, I felt that was okay. Then I began to realise I was in a bad state, I wasn't really interested any longer, and I was doing it because I could. Eventually I just had to knuckle down and say I'm packing up.

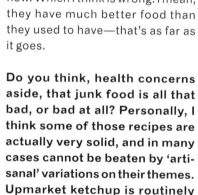

Has much changed in food since then?

I mean, you've got to realise the paucity of the so-called gastronomic revolution. In the second half of the '80s and into the '90s, the gastronomic revolution was something that happened in London, and to a much smaller extent in other big cities. Not that much has changed, I suspect. London obviously has changed, but in a much more general sense it has seceded from the rest of Britain—the capital of Britain should be somewhere like Leamington Spa.

In strictly geographical terms...

Well in geographical terms, Birmingham. But London's culture and so on is completely apart from the rest of Britain. There's no congruence between London and, say, Evesham.

I wonder if our obsession with food is basically a class thing. It's just a way of being elitist.

I don't know if there's anything particularly wrong with elitism in general. If you don't have elitism, you have everything come down to the level of Burger King or KFC. But the secondary point I'd make about that gastronomic revolution is: I started writing for *The Times* in the summer of '86, and within about 18 months Alastair Little had opened, Simon Hopkinson had opened, The River Café had opened and Marco Pierre White had opened. Those places set the template for the next quarter of a century. It was quite an exciting time. But what I would say in general, about food in Britain, is the really successful part of the whole restaurant enterprise is PR. Britain is very good at PR, which is basically selling delusion. And the British delude themselves that they've somehow got the best food in the world now. Which I think is wrong. I mean, they have much better food than they used to have—that's as far as it goes.

Do you think, health concerns aside, that junk food is all that bad, or bad at all? Personally, I think some of those recipes are actually very solid, and in many cases cannot be beaten by 'artisanal' variations on their themes. Upmarket ketchup is routinely disgusting, for instance.

It was pointed out to me at a literary festival a few weeks ago that the characters in my fiction eat appallingly, junk food mostly, with a few people going in for gross excess. This may well give a better impression of what interests me than any number of reports on cute tapas or grand-mère's cassoulet. The word 'artisan' makes me reach for my knuckle duster. But really, I'm indifferent to junk food. It doesn't get me worked up. I haven't eaten a McDo since my youngest

Cité Radieuse, in the first Unité d'Habitation by Le Corbusier
"The building where I live is a very large concrete block—with 334 flats within—
and it's predominantly bourgeois academics, doctors, shrinks, etc., many of whom are
experts in Le Corbusier. It's a beautifully planned building, the idea of 'a machine for living
in' sounds very cold and kind of austere, but in actual fact the flats are anything but.
They're extremely practical, but they also have a kind of warmth. They're weirdly homely."

A mid-century childhood
"It was a curious upbringing. My parents never gave me anything to rebel against,
they never complained my hair was long, or that they didn't like my clothes. They didn't
find my friends unsuitable, even though some of them were definitely unsuitable people.
An Encyclopaedia of Myself is a portrait of mid-century provincial England.
I mean it obviously has something to do with me, but I'm quite an evasive sort of person,
and there's an awful lot that isn't there."

daughter was 12, getting on ten years ago, and I have never eaten KFC, though I used to have an occasional Wimpy back in the day. There's a highly unsanitary looking hole-in-the-wall in Marseille where I buy the most delicious falafel, and I've eaten stuff from street vendors all over Europe, North Africa and South America. Whether or not it qualifies as junk food, I have no idea. I've only once been ill from such grub, in Barcelona in the late '70s. I dislike greasy spoons.

The British seem to be more interested in 'new food' than other nationalities, which keys into what you've written in your autobiography about the cultural cleansing of traditional British food in the post-war period. Since then I guess we've had to be inventive and borrow from various different cultures. We're constantly looking elsewhere for inspiration.

The fact of the matter is, there isn't really any consensus. The gastronomic culture of Britain is centrifugal, but there's no centre to flee from. There are lots of different pockets that coexist in parallel, and don't actually have much influence on each other. You know, fusion food failed. And at the moment you've got all these places doing cicchetti or tapas, at the same time you've got places like St. John, which has now been going for 20 years, and has had a massive influence—actually recovering British food to an extent. You've also got Chinese restaurants that are probably better than anywhere else in Europe—which is not actually saying much—and all these things exist in parallel, not really touching each other. It's like a kind of gastronomic apartheid. It's very different from France. The French attitude to other food cultures is to take those dishes and try to improve them by making them more French, which the British don't do. The British have this belief in authenticity.

I wanted to talk about architecture a bit. How long has this been an interest for you?

It's something that has been with me all my life, and will continue to be with me. Architecture and topography, places and landscape and so on have played a much

greater part in my career than food has. It goes back to my childhood, I suppose. I was extremely interested in buildings, in places, in cityscapes and village-scapes. Whereas food has just been something I like, but it wasn't the predominant thing in my life. Having said that, I'm much more interested in writing about architecture than I am in architecture itself. It's a subject that is very conducive to film, if it's done well. I rue the fact that there is so little architecture on telly, and that food has been turned into light entertainment, with these complete arseholes like that man... what's he called, Greg Wallace? You know, they're just a load of c**ts.

I'm conscious that I've strong-armed you into talking about food, is there anything else you'd like to get off your chest?

I've talked a lot about the autobiography recently because I've been doing various literary festivals—but I mean, basically it's not an autobiography, it's a child's eye view of a '50s and early '60s upbringing in a particular place—Salisbury, whose main industries were the Church and the Cold War, and, unless you actually lived through it, you can't appreciate that the Cold War meant the imminence of nuclear destruction. One felt that one was on the frontline because Salisbury has a huge military community. It's also near the Boscombe Down experimental aeronautical unit and Porton Down, where they developed agents for germ warfare.

Writing *An Encyclopaedia of Myself* was an exercise in memory. After I'd written some bits I'd look things up to expand or give them dates and so on, but basically I just sat there and remembered everything I possibly could. I don't attempt any kind of narrative; it's much more like a collage. Then again, most of my films are very collage-like, and it's a method I feel happy with. Long narratives bore me rigid. I don't like following stories, I hate the imposition of stories on actuality. I prefer random things that do not necessarily link to each other, stuff that's going around in space.

An Encyclopaedia of Myself by Jonathan Meades is available from 4th Estate

After the Night They Raided Minsky's

Photography: Carl Kleiner
Illustration: Jo Ratcliffe

Photography assistant: Andrea Garcia Portoles

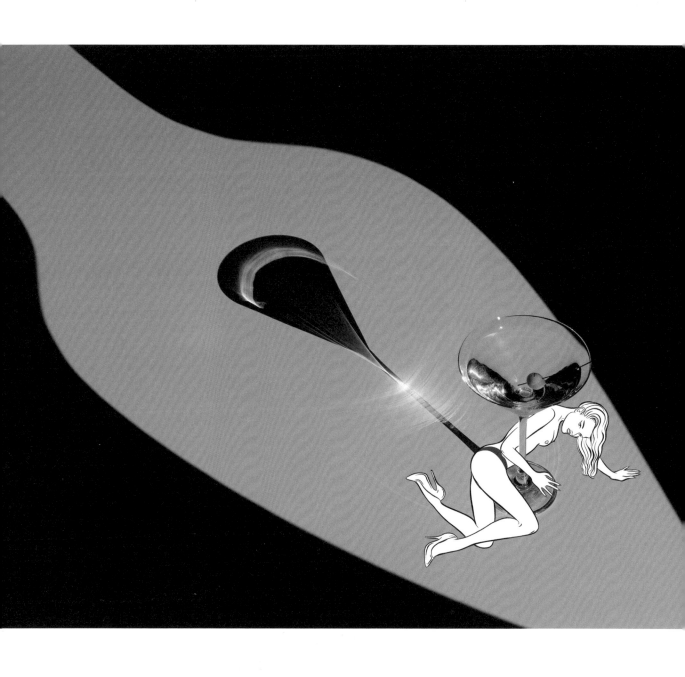

For the RatKleiner Martini recipe → p115

Located in Nagano prefecture, Lake Suwa sits at 760m above sea level, surrounded by the Yatsugatake Mountains. The lake is fed by a vast amount of clear water that flows from the mountains, and it is also a site where hot water gushes out, the second largest spring in Japan. It is here, at Lake Suwa, that the Masumi brewing company has been making sake, enhanced by the mountain water, since 1662. 'Masumi' translates into English as 'genuine transparency'. Sake is brewed for seven months, between October and April. Masumi has two breweries where 30 brewers work, half of which are full-time employees while the others are local farmers. Every year the master brewer selects a particular quality for the sake, deciding on a certain fragrance or flavour, informed by feedback from the previous year's production. This perpetual process ensures that Masumi sake evolves, year after year.

Genuine Transparency

Words: Takamasa Kikuchi
Photography: Julia Grassi

The main ingredients in sake are rice, water, koji mould and sake yeast. One of the most important processes while crafting sake is to make the kamekoji—the rice with the fine fuzz around each grain—an essential ingredient that provides the sugar used by the yeast during fermentation. It is also the sweetness that determines the flavour of the final taste. Koji mould and sake yeast are living ingredients, sensitive to local environmental conditions. The brewers combine scientific observation with an intuitive understanding based on years of experience. For two full days and nights, rice that has been cultivated with koji mould spores is mixed by hand in order to spread heat evenly. After this process, transparent sake is pressed out. Masumi's sake is crafted with the brewers' careful attention.

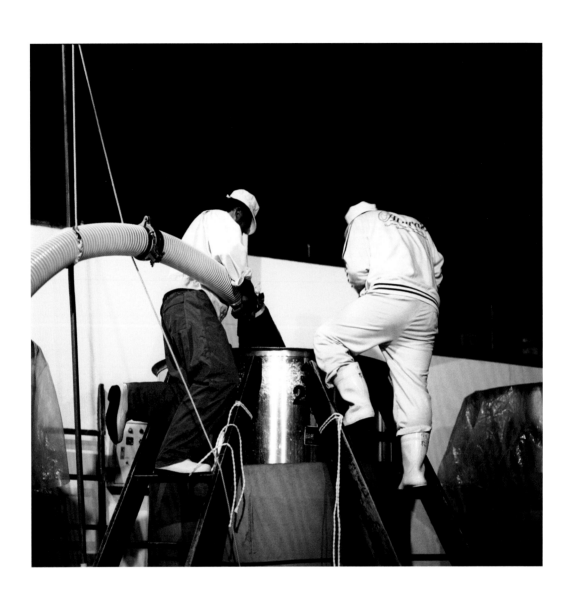

Words: Louise Benson

Celebrity, Scandal and Spectacle

A Family Portrait of Odin's

We had finished dinner by about 9pm. It was midsummer and my dad was peeling peaches for dessert when the phone rang. One hand wiped stickily on a tea towel before I heard him say, "Hello?" There was a pause, and then, "Look out of the window," he said to us, sharply. From our flat on the sixteenth floor of a tower block on the Edgware Road, London sprawled below in miniature. Fanned out directly before us were the narrow, slowly darkening streets of Marylebone, disrupted by the bright, terrifying lights of a blaze...

Watercolour of the view from our
window on the sixteenth floor on Edgware
Road by Patrick Procktor

My dad had grown up here in the late 1960s and 1970s, and his childhood memories could be easily plotted from our aerial view over the neighbourhood. Running past Blagden Fishmongers on Paddington Street to avoid the overpowering scent of warm fish on melting ice, to playing with toy trucks in Moxon Street car park. Then a quaint underdeveloped area, my father told us about sleepy antique shops that had sat alongside a handful of clothing boutiques—a far cry from the upscale bars and sleek design havens that have opened in recent years. Rent was low. It was to Marylebone that my grandma, Kirsten Andersen, had moved from Copenhagen in 1960. And it was here that she opened a restaurant five years later at 26 Devonshire Street. Odin's—so named in a nod to her Nordic heritage.

My dad always liked to guide our line of vision at the window straight ahead to the home where he had spent his childhood and early adulthood, and where my aunt Juliet and uncle Nicky still lived. Nestled behind a black painted door at the end of Manchester Street, the house was clearly visible from our window high up. On the night of the phone call, it was in flames. Orange and immense, with black smoke daubed above, it looked like an impossible painting against the skyline. I was nine years old, and it is an image that I will never forget.

My step-grandad, who also still lived in the Manchester Street house, was a loud, flamboyant artist named Patrick Procktor. Many of his pieces, and those of long-time artist friends, including David Hockney and Francis Bacon, were consumed in the fire. The house had originally been split into two flats. Patrick had lived in one, where he painted his view of the garden, casual still lifes and portraits of the young artist friends and acquaintances that would often come by. In the other had lived my paternal grandparents, Kirsten and James Benson.

From this spot Kirsten and James planned their shared business, opening Odin's as a modern British restaurant that did away with the stuffier graces of many other eateries at the time. As a child I marvelled at the wooden monkeys imported from Denmark that seemed to look mischievously at me as I ate, while the walls remained crowded with artwork, Hockneys and Procktors originally given by the young local artists in exchange for meals.

Mushrooms on brioche was an Odin's signature, the soft base ordered daily from Maison Sagne, a chaotic bakery on Marylebone High Street—now replaced by a limp and sanguine Patisserie Valerie. Shallow wells hollowed out in each inch-thick slice were tightly filled with finely chopped mushroom pâté, before the whole thing was fried in butter. A dish utterly of its time, its presence—well into the millennium—on an otherwise regularly changing menu was a deliciously greasy taste of a more insouciant past.

History is difficult to grasp when you're young, and the successes and tragedies of Odin's blurred before me, its various characters from over the years recalled simply in the delicately painted portraits still printed upon its menus. My grandad James was killed late one night in a crash on Harley Street in 1966 as he drove home. This brought about change when Peter Langan, a local friend and regular diner at the restaurant, arrived one afternoon to find Kirsten, my recently widowed grandma, crying amongst the tables. An imposing Irishman who had bounced from odd job to odd job since arriving in Marylebone, he offered her his help.

Both prized high-quality ingredients prepared simply, presented in good-sized portions and priced well. My grandma gave an equal stake in the business to Peter, and together they worked seven days a week in the cramped basement kitchen, turning out roasted joints of lamb and thick steaks with whipped horseradish sauce, accompanied by rich entrées. A roll-call of the artists, designers and actors of London began to trickle through the doors, many becoming long-term regulars. Ron Kitaj, Ossie Clark, Derek Jarman, Sean Connery—together they brought the high-octane buzz of fame to this small setting.

Peter and my grandma argued loudly and bitterly, but could also share secrets together with great affection. They spent long meals out at other London joints for a regular taste of their competition; neither was formally trained in the restaurant business, giving their own place a relaxed intimacy. Dashes would be made to the local Sainsbury's when they ran out of cream, and dishes were cooked to order at a leisurely pace that would surely have driven any ordinary commercial kitchen out of business.

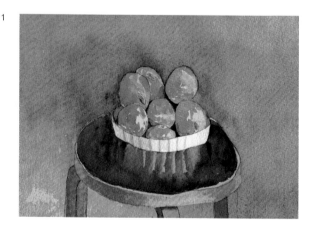

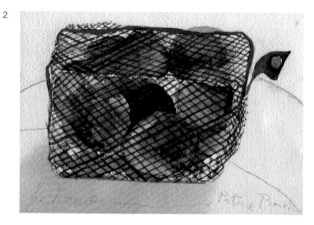

1	Watercolour of a bowl of tangerines at our house by Patrick Procktor	4	Interior of the second, larger branch of Odin's on Devonshire Street	7	My grandma photographed in front of Niagra Falls
2	Watercolour of a punnet of peaches by Patrick Procktor	5	Peter Langan and my grandma	8	Patrick with my dad and aunt Juliet
3	My grandma when she was younger	6	My dad with my uncle Nicky, Manchester Street, Marylebone	9	Patrick outside the Manchester Street house

3

4

5

6

7

8

9

10

11

A glowing review of Odin's from restaurant critic and gossip columnist Quentin Crewe brought queues that spilled out of the tiny, cramped restaurant. This led to the opening of a second branch in 1973, larger and more refined, next door at 27 Devonshire Street. The reception for my grandma's second wedding, to Patrick, her artist-neighbour, was held here. In this, he also took on the role of stepfather to my dad, later becoming the only paternal grandfather that I ever knew. Peter prepared an enormous buffet for the occasion, although a handful of fried oysters taken casually by my grandma from the overflowing table became a darkly comic family tale of her unfortunate wedding-night stomach upset.

The restaurants' reputations have been passed down to me in snatched anecdotes, old photos and paparazzi snaps: Lucien Freud's regular chair, the time Michael Caine almost tripped over me when I was a young child, Peter's gleeful, drunken insults to his famous patrons. At the heart of Odin's, and later its third and most notorious offshoot, Langan's Brasserie, in Mayfair, was a true understanding of the restaurant as a stage for theatre in its purest form. Diners came to participate in the drama.

The Chiltern Firehouse, opened earlier this year, is perhaps the first restaurant with a comparably powerful affinity for the high drama of celebrity, scandal and spectacle. Housed in a former Marylebone fire station, it was, coincidentally, from these vaulted depths that the engines and hoses came to put out the fire at Manchester Street that evening all those years ago. I like to see this as a curious passing of the baton from old to new, particularly since the two original branches of Odin's closed in 2012, their early Hockneys and Procktors swiftly snapped up at auction.

My grandma died in 1984 while she was still young, suddenly and quietly in her sleep. I never knew her, but she has been described to me as laidback and immensely generous. Peter continued to oversee the restaurants with characteristic flair, until his own early death in 1988. Killed in a fire of his own, accidentally started at his home in drunken anger, the flames took with them the last original essence of Odin's and the Brasserie. Both stood for creativity and honesty—and the inevitable bad manners, bad habits and bad endings that these all too often entail. I do hope that traces will remain in Marylebone, still scorching its surface.

For Kirsten Andersen's Morning Buns recipe → p118

10   My aunt Juliet and cousin Giles
11   Patrick and my grandma cutting
      the cake at their wedding reception,
      with Peter Langan on the far right

Words: Kingston Trinder

Images: The Liberace Foundation for the Creative and Performing Arts

Liberace Cooks!

"Seven dining rooms!" Carol Truax, prolific cookbook writer and immensely good friend of Liberace's, roundly exclaimed. "What do you do with seven dining rooms?"

"Come to Hollywood", said Liberace, "and I'll show you". And that is how *Liberace Cooks! Hundreds of Delicious Recipes for You from His Seven Dining Rooms* came to be. It is a sojourn through the piano-playing entertainer's luxurious Hollywood residence, originally published in 1970. Commencing with a chapter entitled, "Indoor–Outdoor Eating", Liberace immediately betrays his Polish and Italian lineage, with generous servings of pierogi and sauerkraut, pot roasts and parmigiana, casseroles and gnocchi, plus carrot and caraway Vichy.

Risotto, fettuccine, artichoke and broiled swordfish all complement such bucolic fare: Liberace's deprivations of yesteryear informing many of these traditional recipes, which were served beneath crystal chandeliers. "Grace is always said before meals", writes Truax. "After the hard times, long ago, Liberace is sincerely thankful for his blessings—and at home, dinners still include mom's specialities."

A chapter entitled, "Do It Yourself and Eat It Yourself in the Kitchen", follows next, an exhaustive anthology of short-order recipes, a stove-to-mouth routine that reflects Liberace's nocturnal nature and the informality with which he entertains, both on and off stage, and all made within what Truax calls the "beautiful... spacious, many-windowed" kitchen, "tiled in gleaming blue and papered in white with figures of the same Delft blue". Owing to the rigours of performance, Liberace's "fifteen minute breakfast" of baked eggs with Parmesan cheese is taken in the late afternoon. However, true reverence is reserved for his spectacular omelettes. "The kitchen is the place

"Liberace possesses a 'favourite sausage routine'. Garlanding one corner of that sumptuous quilted blue leather bar with a spacious sausage table, guests are then assailed with 'great platters of: salami, bologna, tongue sausage, sausage loaf, blutwurst, liverwurst, Braunschweiger, cervelat and head cheese'."

for short orders", writes Truax. "Anyone who respects an omelette wants it made on the spot especially for him, and put before him straight from the pan, to be eaten at once. If this isn't a short order, what is? Each individual omelette is a production, and who stages a production better than the entertainer who is known all over the world as 'Mr Showmanship?'"

The adulated Mr Showmanship, Liberace, or simply Lee, was born Władziu Valentino Liberace, in West Allis, Wisconsin, on 16th May 1919. The second son of Salvatore Liberace, an Italian French-horn player with the Milwaukee Symphony, and Frances Zuchowska, a Polish pianist and Rudolph Valentino enthusiast, the young Władziu's prodigious talents became apparent in his fourth year, when he started playing piano, alongside elder brother George and sister Angelina, and he received a scholarship to the Wisconsin College of Music when he was just seven-and-a-half. According to his autobiography, *Liberace*, the scholarship "lasted seventeen years—the longest the college ever awarded". Educated for over a decade by piano instructor Florence Bettray-Kelly, who, he notes, "liked me, although my career didn't turn out exactly the way she had in mind", Liberace spent his adolescence and the beleaguered years of the Great Depression performing popular arrangements for theatres, Milwaukee radio stations, dance classes, social clubs, weddings and cabarets, under the moniker Walter Busterkeys, and with a high-school band, The Mixers. It was during this time that Liberace's aptitude for gastronomy finds, perhaps, its first expression. "It was the Depression in those days", he recalls. "Mom was a great cook, but she had to go to work, and who was there to make the meals but me? I enjoyed it, I always did like food. Then when The Mixers played for a dance, there'd be a little more money to buy something special to eat."

Something special to eat is certainly to be found within the chapter entitled "Beautiful Buffet by the Yard", an assortment of recipes for stroganoff and salad, chowder and cacciatore, pilaf and paella. Here, Liberace's beloved mother Frances draws greatest note with a sumptuous potato soup, which won the blue ribbon at the Milwaukee Wisconsin State Fair. This then gives forth to the "TV Dining" chapter, a collection of self-contained meals, "the kind of dinner which is all on the table at once. No servants come and go to block the view. Nobody has to jump up and serve himself". And then to "Cookout on the Loggia", a true extravagance in outdoor banqueting, all prepared beneath "a decorative frieze of piano keys". A note of rare temperance attends Truax's survey of Liberace's barbecuing. "When Liberace cooks out, he means business. He doesn't wear his diamonds or his ruffles, nor does he have a candelabra on the outdoor grill. He wears a chef's apron, like

anybody else's—but with a difference—and brandishes a three-foot iron fork." Wise in the ways of appetite, Liberace exploits the art of broiling.

So onward to "Room with a View", a chapter titled after what is perhaps the more practical of Liberace's seven regal supping rooms. The luxurious quarters had a considered purpose, built, as they were, "for the special benefit of his particular friends, the gentlemen of the press". Amply endowed with "an around-the-corner bar of quilted blue leather", here, aside more rarefied saloon fare—"Iranian caviar on ice, flanked by toast points; a crock of portwine Stilton cheese with Fortnum & Mason biscuits; super-colossal olives, huge macadamia nuts, pistachios, mammoth West-Coast pecans"—the "gentlemen of the fourth estate" are further ensnared with an assortment of decadent hors d'oeuvres: French-fried bacon canapés and salami roll-ups, chicken livers and codfish balls, devilled eggs and Roquefort dips, cheese straws and steak tartare, chutney, pâté and Malaysian satay. Unparalleled adoration is, however, accorded to sausages, for which Liberace possesses a "favourite sausage routine". Adorning one corner of that sumptuous quilted blue leather bar with a spacious sausage table, guests are then assailed with "great platters of: salami, bologna, tongue sausage, sausage loaf, blutwurst, liverwurst, Braunschweiger, cervelat and head cheese".

Accompanied by never less than six varieties of both breads and cheeses, the sausage routine also encompasses a self-serving hot tray offering guests "sizzling sausages: bratwurst, blockwurst, blauwurst, weisswurst, beerwurst, knockwurst, col-barse or kolbasa, Vienna sausage, pork sausages, frankfurters, sweet and hot Italian sausage". And should Liberace's ardour for sausages ever prove less than apparent to the reader, Truax's sage pronouncement swiftly dispels any uncertainty: "He is a sausage fan. This is due to growing up in Milwaukee, where sausage is the staff of life."

Liberace's Milwaukee, aside being a fount of ambrosial sausage, also proved instrumental in his abandonment of more formal musical arrangements in favour of a popular–classical amalgam, one he termed "classical music with the boring parts left out". Having long performed classical compositions throughout Wisconsin and the Midwest, Liberace, after playing with the Chicago Symphony Orchestra in January 1940, headed east to New York City. Suffering at first all the attendant rigours and deprivations of fame pursued, Liberace gradually amassed admiration and success across the nation's concert halls and auditoriums, chiefly for that emblematic entwining of classical with lighter musical fare, and no less for his increasing showmanship. Ever refining an elaborate stage appearance and flamboyant

in his autobiography, "I put on a show". Arching ever extravagantly upward across the latter 1950s and into the 1960s, Liberace was, by the 1970s, the world's highest-paid entertainer, earning countless millions while courting royalty and celebrities alike. Garbed habitually in exoticisms—ostrich feathers, mink stoles, elaborate furs and colossal jewellery—he declared these garments "no fancier than those some other groups of men wear on their jobs. Nobody rushes up to a matador as he's leaving the bull ring with two ears and a tail to ask him where he got his suit." However he also acknowledges his attraction to decadence stems from leaner times. "I lived through so many years without having anything", he recalls in the introduction to his cookbook, "that I always promised myself that if I got successful, I'd buy everything I wanted for myself, my family and my friends. And I did, and I do!"

Such decadence characterises the entirety of *Liberace Cooks!* The final remaining chapters proving no exception. "Sauces, Sauces Everywhere" boasts an expansive repertoire of well-honed libations. Tomato, red clam and tartar, Chinese, honey and Texas barbeque, Lorenzo, seafood and Louis, hollandaise, béchamel, mousseline and horseradish. "It's the sauces after all", writes Liberace, "that divide the men from the boys, and separate the gourmets from the guzzlers". Nevertheless, the luxurious crescendo is reserved for an elaborate cornucopia entitled "Seven Dinners in the Formal Dining Room". Attended by a somewhat unexpected atmosphere of rare restraint, despite the grand occasion, our venerable host wears "no suit of lights like a matador's, no diamond necktie, nothing lights up but the candles". Staged around a long oval table seated for 12, garlanded overhead by "a splendid crystal chandelier with twenty-four lights", the table service "gleams with red and gold, and so does the pair of many-branching candelabra".

Served one of seven memorable suppers, fortunate guests may find themselves before generous plates of roast Cornish hen and wild rice stuffing, jellied clamato garni and zuppa Inglese, crab cocktail and crème brûlée, alongside roast turkey with mom's stuffing. Or linguini with white clam sauce and cucumbers in cream, Manhattan Club mushrooms and Italian tomato salad, California artichoke soup and meringue kisses. With all the faultless cultivation and poise of a true entertainer, Liberace saves the very best of his seven suppers for last, and the "Dinner of Seven Nations" is described as the "showpiece of all these formal feasts". Roast prime ribs of Omaha beef with Yorkshire pudding follow delicate slices of prosciutto and melon. Attended by creamed spinach with nutmeg, and cauliflower polonaise, the banquet is crowned finally by Grand Marnier soufflé and Turkish

personage, 1945 saw the debut of that very signifier for Liberace himself: the ornate candelabra. After viewing *A Song To Remember*, a biopic of Polish virtuoso Frédéric Chopin, where candelabras adorn the pianist's instrument, Liberace said to himself: "'If candles make Chopin play that well, I'll have candles on my piano.' So I went out to a little antique shop and bought a brass candelabra for $15 and a quarter's worth of candles and put it up on the piano that evening when I did my act. After that whenever I opened somewhere, reviewers commented on the candelabra."

Westward to Los Angeles now, he chose to describe himself as "Liberace—the most amazing piano virtuoso of the present day." Here, amid the exalted stars of the Hollywood pantheon, Liberace rose to fame at last. Performing for Clark Gable, Gloria Swanson and President Truman, appearing across Las Vegas, at Madison Square Garden, Carnegie Hall and the Hollywood Bowl, Liberace commanded extraordinary sums for his every entrance, either on stage, on television—including the fleeting *The Liberace Show*—or in magazines and films. He also had 200 official fan clubs, and notable performances of the time included those for Pope Pius XII and Queen Elizabeth II, as well as for Nat King Cole and Sammy Davis Jr. "I don't give concerts", he asserts

"When Liberace cooks out, he means business. He doesn't wear his diamonds or his ruffles, nor does he have a candelabra on the outdoor grill. He wears a chef's apron, like anybody else's—but with a difference—and brandishes a three-foot iron fork."

"He would've been fabulous if he were alive today. He'd be on the Food Network. Because if you knew him, all that offstage entertaining with food and drinks and everybody having a good time was just as important as that show on the main stage."

coffee, which, Truax says, should contain "muddy sediment in each cup". As the momentous Dinner of Seven Nations draws to a spectacular close, the last of the guests farewelled, the tableware stowed, the cutlery quietened and the candelabrum lulled, one perhaps finds a suitable parallel with Liberace's own passing. Quartering time between exclusive resorts and a triumvirate of luxurious residences he kept in Las Vegas, Palm Springs and Los Angeles, chauffeured about in a golden Cadillac or mirrored Rolls Royce, the glamorous Mr Showmanship's elaborate costumes, ornate performances and complex choreographies became increasingly extravagant, famously declaring himself "a one-man Disneyland".

One-time Radio City Music Hall Rockette, the gregarious Jody Ghanem, possessed an exceptionally tender lifelong friendship with the charismatic Liberace. Fondly recalling such over Beaujolais and hors d'oeuvres at Las Vegas's Cosmopolitan Hotel, Ghanem recounted both Liberace's invitation to dance alongside his troupe in Las Vegas, in late 1979, and his introduction between her and her late husband, Dr Elias Ghanem, a house physician to several celebrities, including Liberace himself. "Liberace played at my engagement party. Liberace played at my wedding", Ghanem recounts. "Liberace always had a vodka and a cigarette in his hand, and I cannot tell you how just so very vibrant his personality was, not only on stage, but also in personal life." Supping regularly with Liberace, Ghanem's recollections reveal an enduring Mediterranean influence both upon his cuisine and reflected within his gregariousness as a performer and host. Partial to Ghanem's Lebanese mother-in-law's fare, "I know he enjoyed the tabbouleh, the grape leaves, the hummus, the baba ganoush, the labneh", she says, Liberace's banqueting nonetheless occurred around the great, all-American grill.

"He'd have barbeques in the backyard for the Rockettes. He was always entertaining; always wanting to make sure everybody was having a good time. And we did have such a fabulous time. Anything we ate at his house, we shared, flowing champagne, hamburgers, hot dogs, shish kebabs. He had great salads and he truly loved shrimp. He loved food and you could tell."

Declaring food and music "the two best things in life", Liberace's pop–classical music finds parallel, too, in those palatial–kitsch juxtapositions that characterise recipes served, tableware utilised and banqueting experienced in his company. Coupling quintessential American fare with decadent refreshments and accompaniments, the epicurean and the pedestrian were equitably entwined. Ghanem recounts: "Everything was the finest of the finest. Even if you were having a hamburger, he served it on a beautiful plate, the finest china. Real napkins, no paper, real glasses, no plastic, somewhat formal, in a fun way." Liberace's hamburgers themselves illustrate both his decadence and innovation. "I remember those hamburgers, cheddar cheese and scallions", says Ghanem. "It wasn't even popular to stick things in your hamburgers, to blend them with other ingredients." Despite an enduring reverence for more traditional American fare, she remembers that Liberace nevertheless yielded habitually to extravagance. "Beautiful old silver bowls of caviar accompanied by delicate toasts, champagne and shrimp and crab claws, more fancy appetiser styles. Food, even back in the dressing room at the Hilton, wonderful meals after the shows, everything", Ghanem emphasises, "was beyond first class".

Continuing to perform internationally throughout the 1970s and 1980s, while appearing in numerous popular television series, including *The Monkees*, *Batman*, *Here's Lucy*, *The Muppet Show*, *Saturday Night Live* and *The Oprah Winfrey Show*, Liberace gave his final stage performance at New York's Radio City Music Hall on 2nd November 1986. Three months later, on 4th February 1987, a 67-year-old Liberace finally passed away, at his Palm Springs wintertime residence. He succumbed to cytomegalovirus pneumonia, borne of acquired immunodeficiency syndrome, or AIDS, having remained, according to biographer Darden Asbury Pyron, "HIV-positive and symptomatic" from 1985 onwards until his death. Bequeathing his vast estate largely to The Liberace Foundation for the Creative X Performing Arts, in Las Vegas, Liberace lies entombed today within Forest Lawn Memorial Park, at the Hollywood Hills Cemetery, Los Angeles.

Observing Liberace's mastery of audiences, those lavish culinary landscapes he both crafted and imagined, Ghanem notes that neither faded memory nor vacillating taste, nor altered medium, could ever bring about her dearest friend's obsolescence. "He would've been fabulous if he were alive today. He'd be on the Food Network. Because if you knew him, all that offstage entertaining with food and drinks and everybody having a good time was just as important as that show on the main stage. And that was my experience with him, and it's a very big part of my life." For Liberace's immense magnetism and augural adaptability throughout the years—aided perhaps by an indefatigable tenacity—continually enraptured audiences, garnered new admirers and secured lifelong devotees. And even in death, no waning of that epitaphic candelabrum's golden luminescence might ever occur. For the show, after all, must go on.

For Liberace's Special Hamburgers, and Brains in Black Butter recipes → p115 X p116

A Brief History of the Modernist Kitchen

Words: Patrick Baglee

In the late nineteenth century, great thinkers, social reformers and industrialists tinkered with the kitchen in every possible respect, and to varying degrees of success. Then, in the twentieth century, the modernists and appliance manufacturers moved in, making the kitchen a focal point of the machine age—a totem for modernism and a harbour for new gadgets. Today, no conversation about the home can start without discussing the kitchen's many roles and significations.

The Frankfurt kitchen
Image © Büro Aicher (1982)

The publication in 1869 of *The American Woman's Home*, by Catharine E. Beecher and Harriet Beecher Stowe, was a significant moment in the development and organisation of domestic life in North America. Catharine and her sister Harriet (who also wrote *Uncle Tom's Cabin*) laid out in the most comprehensive terms what they described as "A guide to the formation and maintenance of economical, healthful, beautiful, and Christian homes". Over 38 chapters, including advice on "care of the homeless, the helpless, and the vicious", and "the management of young children", they offered guidance on every aspect of domestic life, from contents and configurations to the perils that lie within and remedies for each.

Being among the first to take a close look at kitchens as a distinct part of the structure of the home, these two authors were also early proponents of many ideas we now take for granted. They recommended defined areas for preparing food and clearing up. They thought the addition of a kitchen clock would "secure regularity at meals". They even went as far as to question the amount of attention and money committed to the decor of the average parlour, being somewhat shocked that showy interiors and "an unpainted, gloomy, ill-furnished kitchen" were very often found under the same roof.

The Beechers were not just interested in transforming the homes of people with money. Their drive was for wider social reform. The simple fact was that, in the Western world at least, the kitchen in working-class homes performed—of necessity—multiple functions, and the room would become dingy and unkempt as a result. Where two-room dwellings were the norm, the kitchen would also be a gathering place for all of the home's occupants. If it had a wood-burning stove, the kitchen became not just a place to eat and drink but offered the only reliable source of warmth too. Very often, a single table would be where food was prepared and consumed, and also where visitors would sit, children would do schoolwork and the man of the house would rest at the end of the day. The concept of fixed cupboards, standardised drawer units and a gathering of cutlery and culinary tools remained foreign to most ordinary homes.

Yet more important than the kit and caboodle described by the sisters was the book's promotion of something that couldn't be designed or manufactured, namely the emancipation of women by means of smart domestic thinking. Catharine Beecher had long been an advocate of the role of education in helping women achieve a status within the home—and wider world—that was greater than they were afforded at the time. In clarifying domestic responsibilities, the book provided ideas on systems that would allow the woman of the house to apportion an appropriate amount of time to the tasks she had to perform. It was not so much that the book espoused total freedom from domestic duties

Floor plan of the Frankfurt kitchen
Image © Büro Aicher (1982)

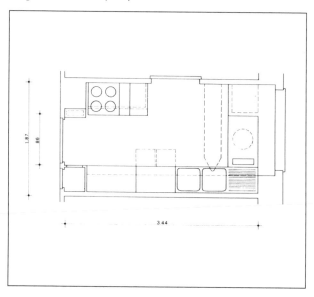

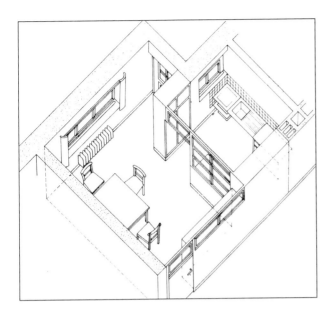

Isometric drawing of the Frankfurt kitchen
Image © Büro Aicher (1982)

but more that, through clever thinking, women would have more free time, and with more free time came the opportunity to pursue activities of self-improvement.

The Beechers' work was revolutionary and its influence far reaching, well beyond domestic confines. Their observation that, in a poorly laid-out kitchen, someone would spend as much time walking between the things they were doing as they would actually doing them reached its apotheosis just over a decade later in the early work of arch streamliner Frederick W. Taylor. Among other things, Taylor was the father of time and motion studies, and committed a good proportion of his working life to the generation and application of systematic thinking about a variety of industrial processes. Eventually known as the discipline of 'scientific management', Taylor's approach was to observe the detail and combination of human and mechanical functions.

The ideas embodied by scientific management faced significant opposition. Many considered Taylor's thinking to be directed at the reduction of workforce numbers. (His desire to remove anything that failed to add value did not sit easily with the emerging labour unions.) But in 1911—and somewhat ahead of his time—he spoke about his work being intended as a means of conserving dwindling natural resources. Taylor was not specifically focusing on how scientific management would impact on the kitchen, but his ideas would prove significant to a new generation of designers and architects, all trying to make sense of a world in the throes of the machine age. In particular, the early modernists would often cite the principles of 'Taylorism' as an important foundation of their quest to reduce the inessential in favour of the functional.

The kitchen was not necessarily a specific target for proto-modernist Adolf Loos either, but the removal of 'stuff' from the home certainly was (if the title of his most powerful published work *Ornament and Crime* was any indication). Loos, who had a noted fondness for Vienna's nightlife, was more properly concerned with distillation. He sought to separate "the necessary from the superfluous components of expression and usage". People took his seminal essay on ornament as a tirade against all decoration, but this rather narrow reading was to ignore a more important and wider point: Loos simply wanted the functional object to have its own inherent beauty, formed by its ability to perform its intended task as simply as possible.

As the nineteenth century came to a close, Loos and his peers began to use machine-age technology to do a few things they'd probably been meaning to get to for a long time—chief among them being to consign the kitchen and its attendant odours to the basement of the home. In particular, the installation of a new-fangled device called the 'dumb waiter' meant that designers and architects could locate kitchens away from living and dining areas (in one of Loos's later buildings, Villa

Müller in Prague, the kitchen was two floors below the dining room). The disenfranchisement of the kitchen was further driven by economic and social factors. For the most part it was affluent clients who commissioned the major modernist houses of the period, and these well-to-do folk (industrialists, bankers, dentists) would almost certainly retain a serving staff. A separate kitchen meant the staff could prepare food away from the gaze of friends, family and society types. These grand homes would form the central portfolio pieces of many a modernist architect, and if they ever considered the kitchen as a place to be used by the actual owner, it was generally as part of competitions to design housing for the working classes. For the most part, their primary focus was on the detail of design and its expression of new materials, as opposed to the Beechers' social reform through domestic order.

As the 1920s unfolded, many designers and architects continued to focus on the rest of the home, opting to let the kitchen take care of itself (or simply hid it underground and out of sight). Yet, as the growing membership of the modernist boys' club continued with their abodes, Austrian architect Margarete Schütte-Lihotzky was busy working on a much more

modest scale, creating what might be regarded as the first truly standardised kitchen layout. Known as the 'Frankfurt kitchen', it was loosely based on the design of a railway dining car. The prototype and eventually the most celebrated variant of it—there would be a Type 1, Type 2 and Type 3—was just 1.9m × 3.4m.

A student of what is now the University of Applied Arts in Vienna, Schütte-Lihotzky was noted for her work on public housing for families, as well as her desire, similar to Catharine Beecher, to consider the wider needs of women and the realities of their lives. The Frankfurt kitchen had been commissioned as part of a social housing programme for its namesake city in the 1920s. In its spare presentation, Schütte-Lihotzky employed different types of surfaces, carefully planned drawer and storage units and built-in appliances. It was as self-contained as any kitchen before it, and designed in such a way as to make it easily replicated in the manufacturing process. It also acknowledged the multiple roles that kitchens performed in more modest dwellings. Rather than try desperately to hide the kitchen, she acknowledged its importance within family life—and, where possible, simply separated it from living areas by means of a sliding door. As much as the work of the grander modernists, it was Schütte-Lihotzky's thinking—from layout to materials—that created a blueprint for the majority of kitchens that followed. Indeed, such is the importance assigned to the Frankfurt kitchen that examples are part of permanent collections in major museums worldwide.

For fairly obvious reasons, any new domestic thinking in the 1930s and 1940s was slow to emerge, but just after the end of World War II, as Europe moved out of austerity, a small furniture business was founded that would have a big impact on kitchens and kitchen design for decades to come. With the 1949 purchase of a sawmill in the the Bavarian town of Bodenkirchen, Martin Bulthaup began the work of building a furniture factory with a focus on great craftsmanship and materials. In those early days the company didn't necessarily consider the whole kitchen, and one of the first products was a single, albeit impressive, cabinet. Then in 1969 they launched Style 75, which was essentially a kitchen cabinet but with multiple sections. In 1974, the C12 kitchen programme presented a far more comprehensive system.

When Bulthaup's son Gerd and daughter Ingeborg took over the running of the company in 1976, Gerd set about looking at the kitchen as more than just a space in which to arrange occasionally related products. A significant factor in this would be the partnership he struck up with design legend Otl Aicher. Founder of the Ulm School of Design, and perhaps best known as the man behind the identity and symbols for the 1972 Munich Summer Olympics, Aicher started working closely with Bulthaup in 1980. He began by redesigning the company's corporate identity but, as someone who thoroughly enjoyed eating and drinking, he couldn't contain himself, and, together with Gerd, he started looking at the kitchen as a unified environment.

It was a powerful partnership. Presenting an Architects Partner Award to Aicher in 2014, a representative from the German Design Council recalled the key principle behind his thinking: "He made it clear that you do not cook facing a wall but rather in the middle of a room, with others, in a dialogue." Such thinking would eventually be gathered in *The Kitchen is for Cooking*, a book into which Aicher poured many of his thoughts on the structure and contents of the home kitchen, and which was in part inspired by research that he had been commissioned to carry out by Bulthaup. The outcome of all this, the kitchen island, would be the next step in liberating greater functional space. In 1988, after the island, their kitchen workbench (the latest version is the b2) was a further expression of Bulthaup's desire to establish a sense of the communal within the kitchen environment by means of liberating things that were once affixed to the wall.

Similar efforts from other manufacturers were happening in parallel. In particular, Hans Hilfiker's work at

Left: Ingeborg Kracht-Rams (wife of Dieter) at the first Vitsoe showroom in Frankfurt, courtesy of Vitsoe Archive
Below: Drawing of the Bulthaup Style 75 cabinet

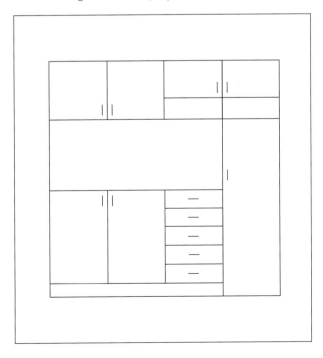

Therma AG would be fundamental to the development of what finally became the Swiss norm for kitchen dimensions. Hilfiker had previously been an employee of the Swiss Federal Railway, and most famously added the red-paddle seconds hand to its railway clock design. He was engaged by Therma AG from 1958 to 1968, and set about working towards a set of consistent dimensions—based on real human interactions with the home environment—as soon as he occupied his new office. As well as proprietary benefits, the standard Hilfiker developed—namely 55cm wide × 60cm deep × 90cm high—would mean manufacturers, appliance designers and architects could work to a consistent set of measurements in a way that hadn't necessarily been possible before; if an appliance broke, you could easily slot in a replacement. Self-evident now, this degree of standardisation was a step forward at the time, and would have long-lasting implications—not the least being the full blossoming of the flat-pack kitchen.

Vitsoe is another famous name that has, to some degree, seen the kitchen as a place for good design. Founded in 1959 by Niels Wiese Vitsoe and Otto Zapf to produce the furniture designs of Dieter Rams, their primary focus was to develop the principle of modular systems, where elements can be introduced, replaced and refined without compromising other aspects. Their 606 Universal Shelving System is indeed a design of considerable merit, although it was Rams, in his primary role as chief design officer at Braun, who would ensure that handsome kitchens were populated by equally handsome and functional small appliances.

There have, of course, been missteps—grand attempts to provide total liberation from the stresses of cooking, or indeed any engagement with the murk and effluvia of culinary life. Fully automated kitchens, where the cook would be required to do nothing but push the correct button, failed to catch on. In the 1950s, Frigidaire presented a kitchen that operated by menu cards. Pop the card for your dish of choice into a slot and all the ingredients are gathered and prepared (by means they didn't necessarily clarify). In the meantime, the lady of the house could pop off for a game of tennis or a spot of golf. At least that was the plan. In fact these utopian visions, born of the all-pervasive spirit of the space age, did little to aid women's liberation. In fact the sight of a liberated woman enjoying these maddening romps shown in advertisements only served to affirm the fact that, to the men who presented these jaunty tableaux, women were still—essentially—kitchen dwellers. Even the otherwise conservative Bulthaup appeared to push the envelope just a little too far with its Type 1 kitchen—essentially a very grand stage for food prepared entirely by microwave oven. Thankfully, true functionality won out over gimmicks, and simplicity trumped the quasi-solutions that sought only patents and profits.

The Bulthaup System b
Image copyright © Bulthaup (1984)

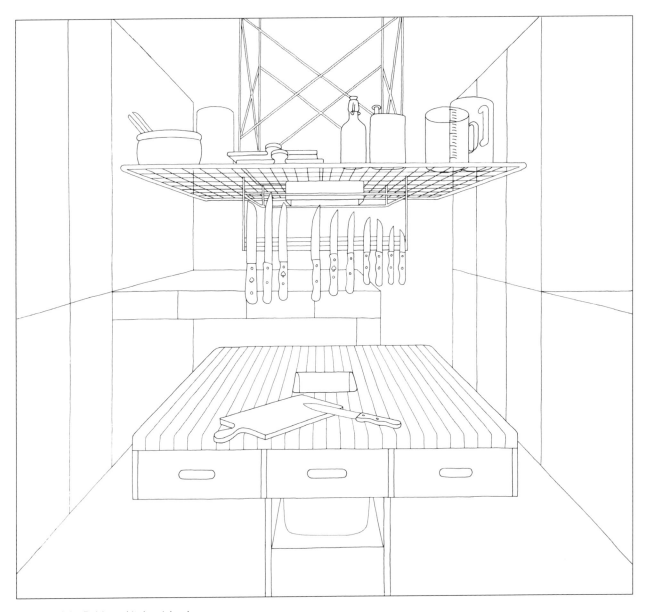

Drawing of the Bulthaup kitchen island
Image © Büro Aicher (1982)

Today, the kitchen seems to have asserted its central position within the wider context of the home, whether in grand houses or otherwise. The Beechers would perhaps not be surprised. Indeed, it is to Catharine Beecher and her sister that the greatest debt is owed for the concept of the kitchen as we understand it today. Almost 150 years ago they established a sense of the home as an entity, and the kitchen's fundamental place within it. They also encouraged women to step away from the responsibilities that they had hitherto shouldered, and expand their horizons. With this began the slow, steady journey of the modern Western kitchen, a place where, now, men and women alike cook, eat and socialise. Irrespective of design, this is surely one of the most important developments in the understanding of domestic life as we experience it today.

ROE

Last year I built an automated camera that—even if just by a little—expands the possibilities of microscopic deep-focus photography. I spent months lurking around online forums populated by retired men who take pictures of bugs and minerals in their sheds. I sourced many a priceless long-working-distance microscope objective from disgruntled Malaysian metallurgy-lab workers, only to put them back on eBay once I found a combination of optics crisper still. The arrangement of lenses and camera components I work with now bumps up against the limits of what visible-spectrum light will resolve. It will take, at a prompt, a sequence of pictures of a subject across a range of focal planes. I then feed these images through software that extrapolates a depth map of the object photographed, and, based on that, collapses the data into one image, unobtainable by optical means alone. In an attempt to turn the tables on the information-age cliché, I enjoy seeing what happens when I overwhelm the machine with inputs. For instance, if I introduce a quality of light that allows for areas of darkness and specular highlights, my algorithms will respond to the uncertainty and variance of the image data by rendering visions of the microscopic sublime that strike me, aesthetically, as quite romantic. The images produced hover between the organic and the virtual; they are evidence of what happens when you try to teach a machine not just to see but to look. I like that. And fish eggs.

**Words & photography:
Ernst Fischer**

For Brad McDonald's Brown Butter Ice Cream and Caviar recipe → p115

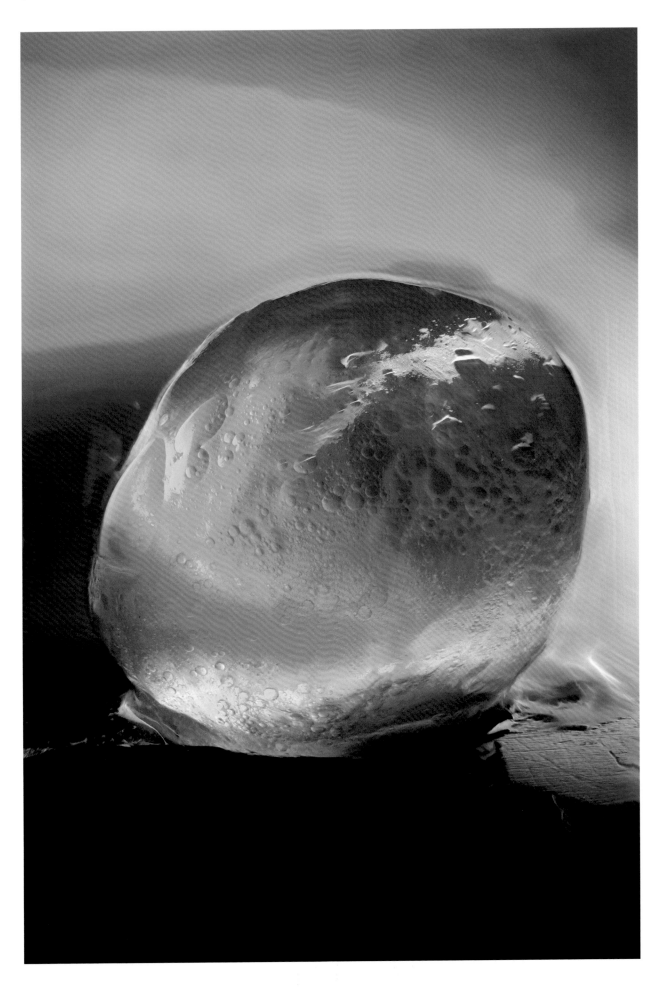

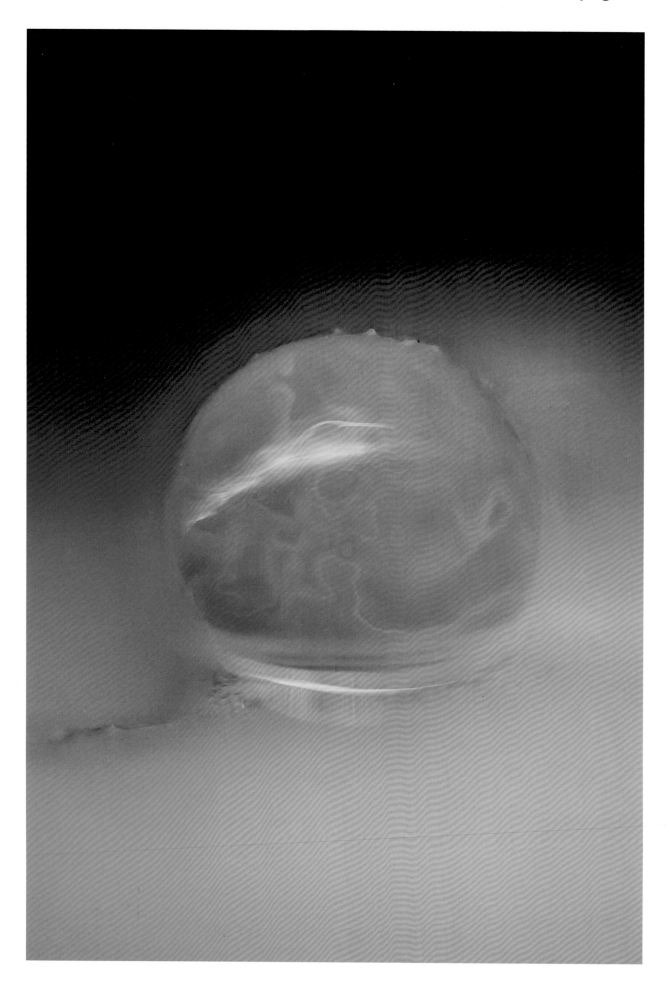

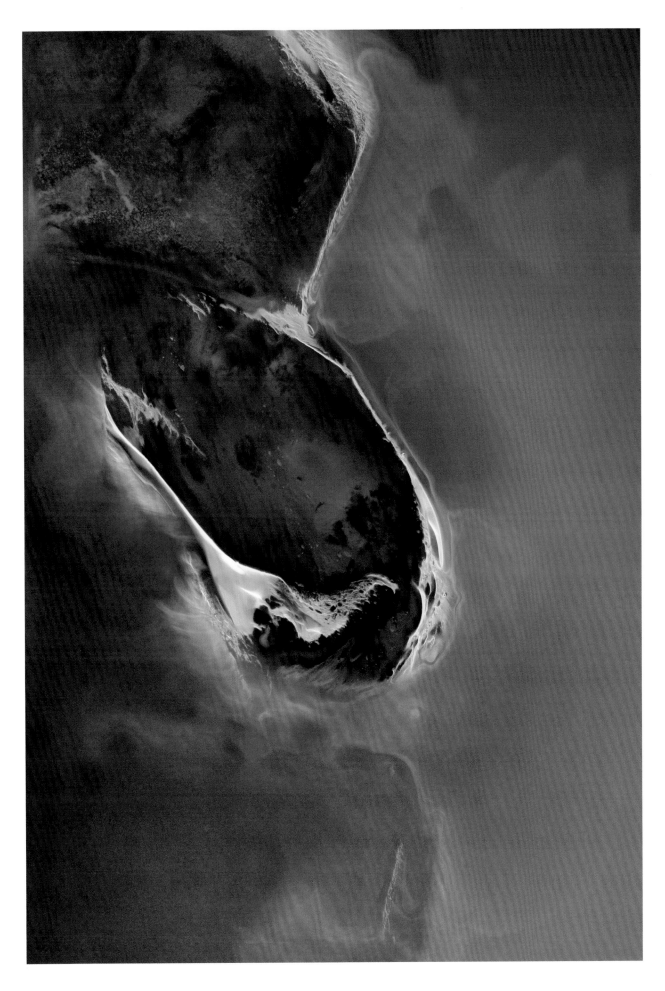

DOG EAT DOG

Concept & Art Direction: *The Gourmand*
Photography: Jess Bonham • Styling: Julian Ganio
Food Styling: Peta O'Brien • Retouching: Passeridae Ltd

Doogie wears
Paul Smith SS15
Navy, Green and
Olive Stripe

Hot dog: British
pork sausage, white
flour square bap,
dill pickle, cara-
melised onion and
English mustard

For Peta O'Brien's
Doogie's Dog recipe
→ p116

Betty wears
Paul Smith SS15
Navy Chevron Stripe

Hot dog: chicken
and beef sausage,
vertical stripes of
ketchup, American
hot mustard and
Marie Rose sauce

Frank wears
Paul Smith SS15
Grey and Blue Spot
Banana Print

Hot dog: pork cock-
tail frankfurter,
brioche roll,
slaw and pickled
red onion

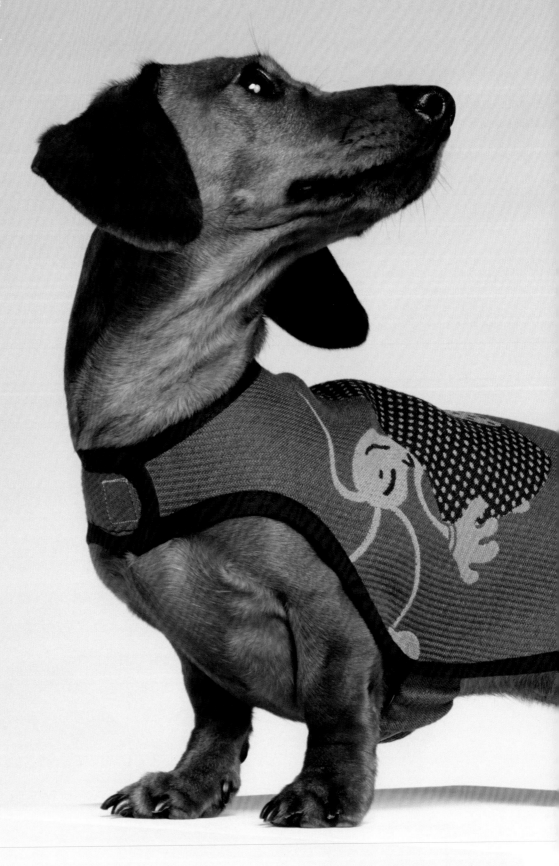

Betsy wears
Paul Smith SS15
Pale Blue Paisley

Hot dog: pork frank-
furter banh mi,
finely cut carrot,
pickled pink ginger,
pickled radish
and Marie Rose sauce

Photography
assistants:
Ben Catchpole
and Andy Price

Food styling
assistant:
Neus Monte Perlas

Styling assistants:
Ogun Gortan and
Rosie Bertuello

Special thanks to
Agi and Sam Studio

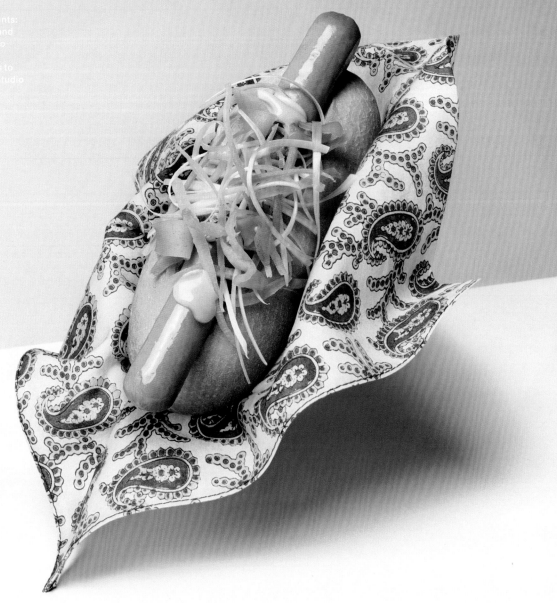

You Are Beautiful... But You Smell of Bacon

Words: Kelly MacLean • Illustration: Tim Lahan

I live in the world capital of veganism: Los Angeles. Here, even Michelin-star-studded chefs cater to the vegan palate. They have to. Vegans now make up roughly 2.5 per cent of the US population, a number that has more than doubled in the last few years. At this rate we could be 80 per cent vegan by 2050. In LA it could happen by Friday.

I'm an animal lover. I particularly love lambs—roasted up with garlic, sea salt and olive oil... But in truth I love living animals too. So much so that I once successfully went cold-turkey vegan, for three whole days until I fell into an anaemic coma and regained consciousness halfway through a Double-Double burger at In-N-Out.

I have yet to try one of the many meatless cafés that have sprouted up recently in LA, and on this sunny Tuesday morning I venture out to observe the virtuous. I'm conspicuous walking into Venice Beach's glamorous vegan hotspot Café Gratitude for two reasons. 1) I've neglected hair and makeup alike. 2) I smell of bacon.

This location is one of several Café Gratitudes— they're sprouting up around the state like California wildfire. I wonder if they all look this shabby chic. The open floor plan and abundance of sunshine create a feeling of warmth, which is reinforced by aspirational words on the walls such as 'Healthy', 'Kind' and 'Spiritual'. The first person I notice is a deeply tanned young man with a white paisley-patterned tattoo ornamenting his face. To his left is a woman with cornflower blue hair, and I feel like I've wandered into The Capitol from *The Hunger Games*.

A supermodel moonlighting as a hostess hides me in the back corner. I look at the menu, which features innovative constructs such as 'chia seed porridge' and 'coconut bacon'. And, yes, kale, kale, kale. To drink I consider a probiotic shot, but at $25 an ounce the aptly named 'I am Outrageous' is out of the question. My second-choice drink arrives promptly, escorted by a buff young man wearing a skin-tight T-shirt. "You are Golden", he says, slipping my drink onto the table. "Thank you", I blush. His responding chuckle triggers a rare brainstorm and I realise that 'Golden' is not so much a comment

on my tangled blonde locks as it is the name of my dairy-free turmeric latté. (Can you even call it a latté at this point?) Every dish is a glorious adjective like 'Beautiful', 'Liberated" and 'Radiant', qualities that the waiting staff attribute to the customer when serving. This is their shtick.

A pale, willowy waitress approaches to take my order. I consider the cashew–cheese nachos and the sprout salad, unconvincingly named 'I am Fulfilled', but decide on 'I am Whole', a bowl of macrobiotic quinoa and veggies. She jots down my order. "And a side of ribeye", I joke. She rolls her eyes and floats off.

The sacrosanct aspect of veganism is perhaps why I've stayed away. Individually they are kindly saints, but, collectively, vegan culture has bred a certain pretension. Sure, they don't harm animals, they don't support a meat industry that, according to the US Food and Agriculture Organization, causes between 14 and 22 per cent of the world's greenhouse gases, and, most importantly, they look fantastic. But the thing is, if you treat us omnivores like something you found on the bottom of your faux-leather boot, you're polluting the planet, too.

The waitress returns with my food. She tells me: "You are Whole", but her eyes say: "You are an Asshole". The dish smells surprisingly delicious. It's composed of quinoa, sweet potatoes, beans, sea vegetables, faux cheese and kimchi (which I will soon discover was specifically designed to have my stomach make whale sounds). Blissfully unaware of this fact now, I take my first bite—it's heaven! The texture is evocative of baby food, but, oh, the flavour. Salty! Sweet! Umami! Fantastic. The knowledge that this ambrosial meal contains no cuddly creatures, no rBGH, no antibiotics, and is friendly to the environment, makes it that much more enjoyable. The clean fuel puts a spring in my step. Will I convert to veganism now? Will I too be a detoxed diva, poster girl for health and compassion? I'm giddy from the possibilities.

Four hours later, I wake up at In-N-Out, Double-Double in hand. I say to myself: "I am Fulfilled".

For a Crazy Delicious Vegan Chocolate Fudge recipe → p117

Zeus und Leda

Create a cocktail of mythical proportions with Finnish chef and spirit maestro Antto Melasniemi's very own foraged gin.

"This drink uses Tenu gin, which I distil in Helsinki, with the Helsinki Distilling Company. The gin is infused with botanicals foraged from the forests of Finland. It'll make you feel like you're lying on a decaying forest floor in autumn, during the first frost: very refreshing and mystical."

80ml Tenu gin
2 tbsp lingonberries
Pinch of fine white caster sugar
80ml still water from the river Tenu
3 dried rosa rugosa petals

Illustration: Klaus Haapaniemi

Crush the lingonberries and sugar in a mixing glass. Add two rose petals and the rest of the ingredients. Shake with ice, double strain and pour into a chilled, elegant glass. Garnish with the remaining rose petals and serve.

Recipes

Symphony of Moist Joy
Sam Bompas
(Taken from *The Flowing Bowl: When and What to Drink*, by William Schmidt, C. L. Webster & Co, 1891)

This gloriously named drink is culled from the bar book of William Schmidt, a late nineteenth-century bartender and veritable Jupiter Olympus of the flowing bowl. Calling himself 'The Only William', he is said to have invented a new cocktail recipe every day.

The Symphony of Moist Joy sits within the family of the poussecafé: highly alcoholic, layered drinks where the varying densities of liqueurs and spirits are used to create a prism of colour. The general principle is to put the densest (most sugary) liquid at the bottom of the glass, and then delicately float successively lighter spirits on its surface.

Now get yourself ready to create an alcoholic oasis in a willing participant's naval (or other handy bodily recess), with the layered spirits providing a thrilling libation for your exploring tongue. This is generally one to saunter into the dawn with.

1 part grenadine (bottom of the glass)
1 part yellow Chartreuse
1 part crème de menthe
1 part cognac

Carefully pour the ingredients (in the order listed) into a bodily recess over the back of a bar spoon, preventing the layers from intermingling. A steady hand and deep belly button is required for assured success.

If you have a particularly hairless and brave volunteer you can give this drink extra finesse. For added flair heat the cognac a tad and set it alight to serve. If you can master this delicious flaming and layered drink on the body of a supine accomplice, you will truly be an accomplished cocktail whisperer!

....

RatKleiner Martini
Ryan Chetiyawardana,
White Lyan and DandeLyan

"A sensuous concoction inspired by Jo Ratcliffe's illustrations."

60ml London dry gin
5ml cherry Heering
10ml lemongrass and green-tea-in-fused bianco vermouth
1 dash orange bitters

Stir all over ice. Strain into a chilled martini glass and garnish with a green olive.

....

Wholesome Kale Salad
Jason Evans, photographer

This is based on something I had at M Café in Los Angeles. I couldn't figure out how they'd made one of my favourite things, and my taste buds had forgotten that it includes some finely chopped shallots, but I came up with this.

Steam a pile of freshly chopped kale until it's wilted but holding its form. Lift the steamer tray out of the pan and pour out the water. Pour some toasted sesame oil into the pan and add a generous dessert spoon of crunchy peanut butter, using the residual heat to melt them together. Sprinkle over with a little freshly ground coarse black pepper to add a few hot, acidic surprises.

Tip the kale back into the pan and turn it over in the melted dressing. Let it cool. Sprinkle lightly with green Tabasco before eating.

I can happily have this on its own for lunch; however, it's also tasty in a pita with a bit of feta. Try a few drops of lime juice or tamari instead of the Tabasco sauce. Flaked almonds are good in this too if they are fresh and sweet.

....

Brown Butter Ice Cream and Caviar
Brad McDonald, head chef,
The Lockhart

429ml milk
100g sugar
47g egg yolks
60g butter
50g dry milk solids
Caviar

Brown 50g of the butter and set aside. Caramelise the milk solids with the remaining 10g of butter, taking care not to let the mixture burn. Combine with the brown butter and set aside.

Cook the milk, sugar and yolks to 80°C. While still warm, add the brown butter and solids. Chill over an ice bath and freeze. Serve with a generous spoonful of caviar.

....

Liberace's Special Hamburgers
From *Liberace Cooks! Recipes From His Seven Dining Rooms*, Doubleday, 1970

"Liberace may have travelled all over, but he remains as American as hamburger. He has a way with ground beef."—Carol Truax

Liberace begins with sirloin, defatted and twice ground. Seasoned with appropriate herbs and some member of the onion family, the raw beef is piled about half an inch thick on halves of hamburger buns. Then it goes into the refrigerator to firm up.

When the guests are ready, the prepared half sandwiches go under the oven broiler. Not a drop of the luscious juice escapes it: it is all caught by the bun underneath. In a few minutes the top is brown, the inside is succulent and rare and the treat is ready to eat. Help yourself from a varied condiment tray. You can eat your hamburger open-face. Heroes can clap two together. All will shout 'Hurray!'

SERVES 12
6 tbsp minced onion
2 tsp butter
4 lb ground sirloin
1 tbsp Worcestershire sauce
½ tsp oregano
1 tsp leaf thyme
1½ tsp salt
½ tsp freshly ground pepper
6 round hamburger buns

Sauté the onion in butter until light brown. Mix with the remaining ingredients except the buns. Split the buns and put a ½ to ¾-inch patty on the split side of the buns. Put the meat all the way to the edge. Store in a refrigerator to firm the beef until ready to cook. Broil 6 inches away from the heat for 6–8 minutes.

....

Grouse, Bread Sauce and Pickled Mulberries
James Lowe, head chef, Lyle's

Grouse is seen by many as the king of the game birds, and for me it's a sign that the game season has really begun. The first shoot of the year is on 12th August (the Glorious Twelfth), and from then onwards another bird comes into season every month or so. You'll find nature almost writing the menu for you as the next bird and then the next appears, all to be cooked and served to your guests.

SERVES 4
2 onions
8 cloves
1 bay leaf
500ml milk
150g white breadcrumbs
200g mulberries
300g red wine vinegar
150g sugar
1 grouse
Butter
Small piece of sourdough toast
Salt

Cut two onions in half: thinly slice one and stud the other with the cloves. Put the onions in a small pot with the bay leaf, milk and a pinch of salt.

Bring the mixture to a very low simmer, take off the heat and then leave to infuse for an hour. Remove the onion, cloves and bay leaf, and then heat the milk very gently with the breadcrumbs. Stir every 15 minutes until the mixture thickens to the consistency of a loose mashed potato.

Bring the vinegar and sugar to the boil and add the mulberries. Take off the heat and allow to cool. Remove the grouse's head and wings. Cut around the bird's leg with a sharp blade. Cut open the cavity at the bottom of the breastbone and remove the bird's guts, setting aside the heart and liver. Season with salt. Add butter to a heavy-based frying pan. Sear the bird on all sides, starting with the grouse on its side to ensure you coat all surfaces evenly. The bird should brown, not blacken. If it turns black your butter's too hot, if it's not brown enough your heat is too low.

Place the pan and the bird in an oven at 180°C for 5 minutes. When you take it out, test that the thickest part of the breast has reached a temperature of 56°C.

Remove the bird from the pan. Fry the liver and heart in the pan briefly until they begin to firm up, and the bread until it becomes crispy. Leave aside to rest.

Place the grouse breast and leg on the plate. Chop the livers roughly and season with salt, pepper and

grated nutmeg. Spread onto the toast. Plate the bread sauce and add the pickled mulberries to the juice from the pan and spoon over the meat.

....

Brains in Black Butter
From *Liberace Cooks! Recipes From His Seven Dining Rooms*, Doubleday, 1970

SERVES 8
2.5 lb calves' brains (4 pairs)
Salt
Flour
¼ cup butter
Lemon juice or vinegar

Put the brains in a quart of cold water with 2 tbsp of salt for at least an hour. Cook gently in salted water or broth for 15 minutes and plunge into ice water. Remove the membrane—it's easier to do now than before you boil them. Dredge the brains lightly with flour. Heat the butter until dark brown. Add a few drops of lemon juice or vinegar and sauté the brains until they are light brown. Sprinkle with about ½ tsp of salt, and pour the foamy butter over.

....

Doogie's Dog
Peta O'Brien, food stylist

SERVES 1 HUNGRY DOG
1 onion
1 bratwurst
1 gherkin
1 soft white bap
1 tsp English mustard

Slice one medium-sized onion into rings. In a heavy-based frying pan, slowly caramelise the onions until golden. Put to one side but keep warm.

Take a plump bratwurst sausage and pan fry until toasty brown. Make a slit along the top of a soft, floury, white bap and add the hot bratwurst.

Cut a sliced, pickled gherkin in two and place at either end of the sausage.

Pile high with warm, unctuous onions and a good dollop of hot English mustard. Woof!

Cornflake Tart

Simon Gregory,
executive chef, Hoi Polloi

SERVES 12
FOR THE FILLING:
600g golden syrup
600g honey
300g ground cornflakes
4 eggs
300g white breadcrumbs
600ml double cream
Extra cornflakes for the top

FOR THE PASTRY:
625g flour
250g cold cubed butter
250g icing sugar
3 eggs

Heat the honey and golden syrup. In a separate bowl mix the eggs and cream, and blend together the breadcrumbs and cornflakes. Fold all ingredients together and allow to rest overnight.

Mix the flour and butter to a crumb. Add the eggs and icing sugar, and stir together. Wrap the pastry in cling film and allow to rest for 30 minutes before rolling. Roll the pastry out to 3mm thickness, and line the tart case.

Fill the pastry with the filling and then cover the top of the tart with extra cornflakes. Bake at 160°C for around 40 minutes. Remove from the oven, allow to cool, slice into wedges and serve with a scoop of (ideally honey) ice cream.

Peanut Butter Parfait with Toasted Frosties

Jackson Berg, head chef,
Bistrotheque

FOR THE PARFAIT:
8 egg yolks
200g sugar
150ml water
100g peanut butter
800g whipped cream
Zest of 2 lemons
Frosties
Icing sugar

Whisk the yolks for 10 minutes in a mixer until they triple in size and hold a figure of 8. While your eggs are in the mixer, melt the sugar and the lemon zest with the water until it reaches 118°C. Pour this gently into the egg-yolk mix. Then add the peanut butter, and continue to mix until the mixing bowl feels cooler on the outside. Whip your cream to a stiff peak, then fold in the yolk and peanut-butter mix. Line a terrine mould with cling film twice, and add your mix. It's best left in the fridge overnight to set.

FOR THE TOASTED FROSTIES:
Lay a generous handful of Frosties on a baking tray, and dust with icing sugar. Toast in the oven for 5 minutes at 170°C. Once cool, crush the Frosties with your hand and scatter over the top of a freshly sliced serving of parfait.

Best served with a large glass of full-fat milk.

Crazy Delicious Vegan Chocolate Fudge

Kelly MacLean (but courtesy of ohmyveggies.com)

"As my pocketbook and thighs will attest, this recipe for vegan fudge is both more expensive and more fattening than regular fudge, but it is surprisingly also more delicious."

½ cup raw cacao powder
½ cup coconut oil (room temperature, not melted)
¼ cup raw hazelnuts
¼ cup + 2 tbsp maple syrup
1 tsp vanilla extract
Fleur de sel or cacao nibs for topping (optional)

Combine all of the ingredients in your food processor, and mix until completely smooth. This might take several minutes, kind of like when you make nut butter. Be patient! Transfer the fudge mixture to a small, rectangular baking dish that's been lined with parchment paper, and use a spatula to spread it in an even layer. Sprinkle the top with fleur de sel or cacao nibs, if using. Refrigerate until solid, then remove the fudge from the baking dish and cut into squares.

Mabel's Beet and Dark Chocolate Cake

A recipe from
Neneh Cherry's kitchen

3 or 4 beetroots peeled and grated
200g dark chocolate
200–400g of ground almonds
2 eggs
2 tsp of baking powder
200g of coconut sugar
Splash of milk

Mix everything and bake for 15–30 minutes at 180°C.

From Florence White's *Good Things in England*, 1932

FLUMMERY (CHESHIRE), 1615–1895

As 'flummery' and 'frumenty' are sometimes confused (even by the learned who should know better) it is necessary to introduce this old English dish with a few words of explanation.

Gervase Markham writing on 'Skill in Oatmeal' in 1615, says: "lastly from this small oatmeal, by oft steeping it in water and cleansing it and then boyling it to a thick and stiff jelly, is made that excellent dish of meat which is so esteemed of in the west parts of this kingdom, which they call in Cheshire and Lancashire Flamery or flummery...

'Some eat it with honey which is reputed the best sauce; some with wine, either sack, claret, or white; some with strong beer or strong ale, and some with milk."

And Dr Thudichum, one of our greatest authorities on the history, science and practical import of the art of cookery says:

"Flammery signifies an acid jelly made originally from the husks of oats; in Scotland it is known as Sowans. The name is now applied to any starch jelly made from cereals, wheat flour, rice, ground rice, sago, potatoes, etc., the liquid used to develop it being either fruit juice, milk, or even cream."

OATMEAL FLUMMERY, 1823

1. Steep in cold water, for a day and a night three large handfuls of very fine oatmeal.
2. Add as much more water, and let it stand the same time.
3. Strain it through a fine hair sieve, and boil it till it is as thick as hasty pudding, stirring it well all the time.
4. When first strained, put to it one large spoonful of white sugar, and two of orange flower water.
5. Pour it into shallow dishes, and serve it up with wine; or it will be very good with cream and sugar.

RICE FLUMMERY, 1826

1. Boil with a pint of new milk, a bit of lemon-peel, and cinnamon to sweeten it.
2. Mix with a little cold milk 3oz of ground rice.
3. Stir it into the boiling milk, flavour with almonds, add a bit of butter.
4. Boil till it thickens (stirring all the time) and leaves the sides of the saucepan.
5. Pour it into a mould and leave till cold.
6. Turn it out and serve with cream or custard, or stewed fruit, or any kind of sweet preserve.

HOW TO MAKE GOOD TOAST

1. Cut the bread (which must be at least a day old) in level slices, about ¼ inch thick.
2. Dry each side before allowing it to brown.
3. Then brown each side.
4. Put each slice as it is done into a toast rack.

N.B – it is worth noting that very good toast can be made on a Scotch girdle over a gas ring, or a wood fire, or an oil stove, or any other suitable heat.

....

Foaming Lemonade Macarons
By Luke Evans, artist and photographer

"Unassuming at first, the chemistry involved in these macarons will lead to a surprising, zesty foam to fill your mouth once eaten."

YIELDS 30 MACARONS

FOR THE MACARON SHELLS:
100g blanched almonds, ground
175g icing sugar
100g aged* egg whites, room temperature
¼ tsp cream of tartar
40g caster sugar
1½ tbsp yellow food-colouring powder
*Let stand, covered, for at least 24 hours.

FOR THE FILLING:
250g very thick, fresh lemon curd
Icing sugar
Bicarbonate of soda
Citric acid powder

Line three flat baking sheets with silicon paper.

In a food processor, blitz the almonds and icing sugar together to a dry, fine powder.

In a spotlessly clean stand mixer, whisk the aged egg whites and cream of tartar together at medium-high speed until foamy. Whilst continuing to whisk, gradually add in the caster sugar. Whisk to stiff peaks. Briefly whisk in the powdered food colouring.

Sift the almond–sugar powder over the meringue.

Begin the macaronage by beating the mixture vigorously with a thin, flexible spatula for 5 seconds. Now, using a folding action, continue to mix the batter until it slowly falls in a single, thick ribbon. Be careful to not over-beat: it should only be fluid

enough that the ribbon melts back into itself after 20 seconds. This should take about 20 folds after the initial beating.

Fill a large pastry bag with the macaron mix. Using a 1cm plain tip, pipe 1.5 inch rounds onto the baking sheets.

Firmly bang each tray five times onto a table. Leave to stand uncovered at room temperature for 30–60 minutes, until the surface of each macaron is no longer tacky to the touch. Meanwhile, pre-heat the oven to 180°C.

Bake each sheet for 14–16 minutes. Leave to cool.

To assemble, dust the underside of one shell with acetic acid powder using a brush, then pipe the lemon curd filling on top. Dust the underside of another shell with bicarbonate of soda, then with icing sugar. Press the two shells together.

Serve immediately.

....

Morning Buns
Kirsten Andersen, from the Odin's archive

250g flour
½ tsp salt
1 tbsp sugar
20g yeast
1½ eggs
50ml milk
50ml lukewarm water
50g margarine

Crumble the margarine into the flour, salt and sugar. Dissolve the yeast into the lukewarm water and milk, then add the egg. Add this mixture to the dough. Let the dough prove for 30 minutes. Use two teaspoons to shape the dough into buns, and leave to prove for a further 15 minutes. Bake for around 10 minutes at 190°C.

....

ALL THE WORLD WILL BE IN LOVE BE WITH NIGHT

Ace Hotel
London
Shoreditch

acehotel.com

Good Things in England
Florence White (1932)

Words: Ben Houston

In the England of the late 1920s and early 1930s it was widely agreed: good food was French food. English cooking, or at least what little the public (and many vocal food critics) knew of it, was tired, boiled, tasteless and thoroughly Victorian. One thing was certain: it had no place in the exciting modernity of the twentieth century.

It was a 69-year-old cookery writer, journalist and cook-housekeeper who, using borrowed pots and pans in her basement room in Chelsea, was to change this perception forever.

Florence White, frustrated by the mocking misrepresentation of English cooking, and certain that she must rescue "the finest cookery in the world... nearly lost by neglect", set out on an epic journey to reveal the rich English cooking traditions of real people from 1399 —the time of Chaucer—to 1932.

Having herself learnt "good epicurean country-house cookery... handed down the family from mother to daughter since the days of Queen Elizabeth", White understood perfectly that the lifeblood of English cooking far preceded Mrs Beaton and the Victorian obsession with boiling cabbage. Instead, it existed in techniques handed down from generation to generation, a noble thread of English recipes enriched by countless regional divergences; an oral tradition stretching back centuries.

In 1928 White founded the English Folk Cookery Association and began to seek out recipes and cooking techniques from people throughout the country. Travelling from town to town, notebook in hand, and placing adverts in newspapers requesting "local knowledge", she began to build the vast archive that would culminate in her grand manifesto, published in 1932 by Jonathan Cape, under the achingly humble title *Good Things in England*.

The volume is a treasure trove of 853 pointedly economical recipes, few more than 15 lines long. Alongside these, and useful techniques, are astonishingly comprehensive accounts of regional diversities. It is the sheer wealth of this local knowledge that marks the volume out as something

beyond a traditional 'receipt' book, and what can seem unnecessarily specific at first glance ("How to make good toast", for example) is rendered rare in its universality when placed alongside the 11 differing recipes for gingerbread.

The result of her unique and immense exploration is nothing short of a reclamation of the history of English cooking, and this is one of the few scholarly works that can be genuinely considered a practical 'everyday' guide.

The book was a commercial success at the time and remained a staple for some decades, with Elizabeth David referencing the work in the 1950s and Jane Grigson as late as the 1970s. However, by then the general public's interest had waned, and the book fell out of print in 1962, the shadow of obscurity looming. Thankfully the eagle eyes of Persephone Books picked it up in 1999, and they have kept it available ever since.

To have this important work in print is, of course, a joy, but Florence White deserves more. Kate Colquhun in *Taste*, her important study of the history of British cooking, placed White alongside George Orwell as a campaigner in the fight against the growing blandness of homogenised convenience food. More recently, Alexandra Harris included White as one of her band of 'romantic moderns', mentioned in her 2010 book of the same name, all of whom were seeking out authenticity in modernity while savouring traditional knowledge.

Florence White's influence on English cooking aside, her importance in presenting the rich folk history of England in a practical and visceral way ought to place her amongst the great social historians of modern England. As interest in traditional English cooking continues to grow, let us hope interest in such neglected figures grows alongside it, and that, in more ways than Ms White could ever have intended, England can once again truly 'know her wealth'.

Peter Harrington have for sale a selection of rare Florence White first editions, including *Good Things in England*, available at their London shops and online at peterharrington.co.uk